MANAGING CHALLENGING BEHAVIOUR

IN THE CLASSROOM

A Framework for Teachers and SENCOs

Gary Lavan

Routledge
Taylor & Francis Group

LONDON AND NEW YORK

"for Gillian, Olivia & Jack"

MANAGING CHALLENGING BEHAVIOUR IN THE CLASSROOM

For teachers and SENCOs in all settings, this invaluable resource will guide you through a simple, systematic process of understanding why challenging behaviour is happening and give you some very practical, easily implemented strategies that all staff can use to help make things easier for the young people in your group. Key features include: a wide selection of different strategies for coping with challenging behaviour so that you can meet the needs of each individual pupil; a flexible framework with templates and tools to help you proactively plan approaches to challenging behaviour so that you and your colleagues can respond consistently and effectively; and approaches brought to you by an experienced Educational Psychologist, based on proven strategies developed through years of practice in Special Schools as well as Primary and Secondary mainstream schools. Unlike other books addressing challenging behaviour, this resource offers a psychologically based framework that can easily be implemented by mainstream teachers and SENCOs. It works!

Dr Gary Lavan is a Chartered Educational Psychologist and the director of Your Psychology Ltd. He specialises in supporting young people with learning difficulties and challenging behaviour.

MANAGING CHALLENGING BEHAVIOUR IN THE CLASSROOM

A Framework for Teachers and SENCOs

GARY LAVAN

Routledge
Taylor & Francis Group

LONDON AND NEW YORK

First published 2018
by Routledge
2 Park Square, Milton Park, Abingdon, Oxon OX14 4RN

and by Routledge
711 Third Avenue, New York, NY 10017

Routledge is an imprint of the Taylor & Francis Group, an informa business

© 2018 Gary Lavan

British Library Cataloguing-in-Publication Data
A catalogue record for this book is available from the British Library

Library of Congress Cataloging-in-Publication Data
A catalog record for this book has been requested

Visit the eResources: www.routledge.com/9781911186120

ISBN: 978-1-911186-12-0 (pbk)
ISBN: 978-1-315-17419-8 (ebk)

Typeset in Signa
by Apex CoVantage, LLC

Printed in Great Britain by Ashford Colour Press Ltd.

CONTENTS

Chapters 1–2 The first challenge is to understand challenging behaviour. To do so, we will examine:

- Some **evolutionary** and biological explanations for challenging behaviour
- An **Iceberg Model** of challenging behaviour
- A **flowchart** for exploring why behaviour happens and some possible strategy starting points
- The **Challenging Behaviour Cycle**
- The **Coping Plan** document

Chapter 3 The most important phase for developing support is the Yellow Phase. It is here that staff can develop the **preventative** and **Proactive Strategies** that will ultimately help the young person to develop **new coping skills** and prevent the need for the young person to engage in challenging behaviour to have their needs met.

Chapter 4 In the Green Phase we will explore **Focussed Support Strategies** and how staff can **intervene** when unwanted behaviour begins to present. At this phase we will highlight the importance of **spotting patterns of behaviour**, recording these, and analysing them so that we can be more proactive in the future and use the knowledge from these patterns to inform our understanding of the behaviour.

Chapter 5 We will then look at what to do in the Red Phase, when challenging behaviour reaches peak levels. The priority of any **Reactive Strategies** at this phase is to restore order quickly and keep everybody safe if behaviour becomes dangerous.

Chapter 6 After incidents of challenging behaviour, both the young person and staff will need the opportunity to do some purposeful **reflection** and planning about how things might be improved in the future. In the Blue Phase we will look at how to ensure that we adhere to the principles of an **assess-plan-do-review** approach.

Chapter 7 We will reflect on the process of using the Coping Plan, and explore how the Coping Plan fits with other sources of support for challenging behaviour.

ACKNOWLEDGEMENTS

'I feel exceptionally lucky to be working as an educational and child psychologist – doing a job which I truly enjoy. I would like to thank all of the staff, parents, carers, and young people I have worked with in schools in Wolverhampton and the West Midlands over the past decade for all that they teach me on a daily basis. Special thanks go to staff and colleagues, parents, carers, and young people I have had the pleasure of working alongside at Tettenhall Wood School and Green Park School – the most wonderful people'.

CHAPTER I

UNDERSTANDING THE CHALLENGE

Successfully supporting pupils who present with unwanted behaviour in school is one of the most challenging aspects of teaching and education. The framework, approaches, and strategies outlined in this book have developed over many years of experience in classrooms in special school and mainstream school settings, supporting pupils in primary and secondary phases whose behaviour could be described as severe as well as pupils who present with more 'low-level' disruptive behaviours. The book draws upon my own experience as a practitioner psychologist, the experience of staff and parents with whom I have had the pleasure of working alongside and learning so much from, and from the research and literature within the many fields related to positive behaviour support. Specifically, the framework we are going to explore in this book, and the many strategies which are discussed, are grounded in the principles of 'positive behaviour support' – drawing upon a well-established and growing field of intervention research.

Some of the ideas and strategies may be new to you, some of them you may have encountered before. The strategies outlined here are not all uniquely my own – they are drawn from a range of sources and experiences. The framework that we will explore draws much of the knowledge accumulated in the literature into a simple and coherent framework that supporting adults can use to inform their support plans and structure the interventions and strategies they put in place.

This book is not, however, in itself a 'programme' or an 'intervention'. Although heavily informed and underpinned by research, it is not an 'academic' text. It is intended to be a framework and a **practical guide**, to provide you as staff with ways, firstly, to make sense of and understand unwanted behaviour and then to provide starting points for planning how to support the young person effectively.

The framework that we are going to explore is built upon two fundamental assumptions about unwanted behaviour:

1. The first fundamental assumption made within this book is that **all behaviour occurs for a reason**. The assumption is that *all* behaviour *always* serves a function for the young person, without exception. Unwanted behaviour is no different, and it results from an interaction between the young person and the social or environmental demands placed upon them.

2. The second fundamental assumption for this book is that any system of behaviour management which is implemented effectively should have, as its primary focus, the intention of *helping young people to cope* with the things they find stressful in their environment and to **learn ways to manage their own behaviour** with as little adult intervention as possible.

The aim of any support, or intervention, for young people presenting challenging behaviour should be to improve their quality of life (DoH, 2009). This book and the framework described are both designed to support staff to make effective changes to help young people cope better, improve their experience of school, and ultimately improve their quality of life. It is also intended to make the process of supporting challenging behaviour a more manageable endeavour by simplifying the process, making the process more systematic, and helping you to focus on the process that both yourself and the young person are going through.

The framework and the book are broken down into distinct 'phases' which will walk you through:

1. Understanding how to understand challenging behaviour in general

2. Generating an explanation for the unwanted behaviour of individual pupils

3. Planning Proactive Strategies to reduce the likelihood of unwanted behaviour

4. Planning Reactive Strategies to effectively manage difficult situations

5. Reflecting upon and making changes to the plans you have in place

This first chapter sets the context for the framework we are going to use. It is devoted to exploring the complexity of challenging behaviour, and the questions that staff

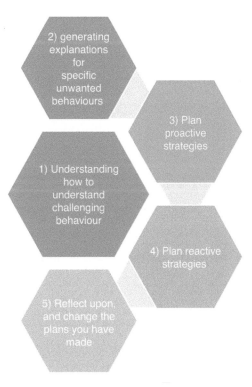

Figure 1.1 Phases of responding

often ask when faced with pupil behaviour which is difficult to manage, including the essential question, '*Why does challenging behaviour occur?*'

In answering this question we will examine the **five underlying reasons** for all challenging behaviour, and provide hope that there are some simple and practical steps that can be taken to help the young person cope with situations better and to learn ways to manage their own behaviour.

At the end of the chapter, **a flowchart** is presented that can be used as a starting point when trying to understand the underlying reasons why a pupil is presenting with challenging behaviour and deciding what strategies and changes might be necessary and helpful for them.

Furthermore, we will learn how to capture all our knowledge and understanding about an individual's behaviour on a **1-page summary document – the Coping Plan** – to help you summarise what is happening and what you as supporting adults have agreed to do in response to the unwanted behaviour being presented.

TERMINOLOGY AND DEFINITIONS OF CHALLENGING BEHAVIOUR

The term '**challenging behaviour**' is used throughout this book to describe any number of behaviours presented by pupils in schools that prove difficult for staff to manage. It is a popular term used widely within the literature, although the pupils to whom it refers are diverse and their behaviours and personal qualities are varied.

You may work with pupils with recognised labels, diagnoses, and identifications such as ADHD (Attention Deficit Hyperactivity Disorder), Autism, ODD (Oppositional Defiance Disorder), Attachment Disorder, Learning Difficulty/Disability, and many others. Equally, you may work with pupils who present with unwanted behaviours in school yet have no such label identifying any such condition. It is beyond the scope of this book to explore the distinctions, merits, and pitfalls of these terms of reference. The framework described in this book is intended to be useful for any staff who are faced with challenging behaviour, regardless of the identification or not of any conditions such as those mentioned above.

Often, within research literature, the term 'challenging behaviour' is reserved for behaviour expressed by young people with severe learning difficulties. Challenging behaviour in this context can be defined as:

> Culturally abnormal behaviour(s) of such an intensity, frequency or duration that the physical safety of the person or others is likely to be placed in serious jeopardy, or behaviour which is likely to seriously limit use of, or result in the person being denied access to, ordinary community facilities.
>
> *(Emerson, 1995)*

The term 'challenging behaviour' used throughout this book refers much more broadly to any behaviour which presents difficulties for staff to manage within mainstream schools and special school settings. Within all of these settings teachers and support staff can encounter behaviours which place the safety of people in danger, or which reduce access by the young person to community facilities, including their school and the curriculum on offer. Behaviour such as this may be part of an established repertoire of behaviour for that young person, or it may be a new and relatively short-term development in response to some changes experienced by the young person.

For the purposes of this book, and the framework described, challenging behaviours can range from low-level disruptive behaviours such as noise-making, refusing to work, and wandering, to more extreme behaviours, including being physically aggressive, damaging property, and self-injurious behaviour. If any of these behaviours exist, either in the short-term or the long-term, then the term 'challenging behaviour' may be used to describe them.

Regardless of the reason or the longevity, disruptive behaviours such as this are unwanted within the context of school environments, and as such you will also find the term 'unwanted behaviours' is used within this book.

UNDERSTANDING HOW TO UNDERSTAND CHALLENGING BEHAVIOUR

We are going to very briefly talk here about the brain. It is beyond the scope of this book to go into any detail about neuropsychology and the intimate workings of the developing brain, and indeed this is not necessary for using the framework set out in this book. However, an understanding of what is happening inside the brain, at a biological and chemical level, when people engage in challenging behaviour (or any behaviour for that matter!) is very helpful when we are trying to plan support for a young person in our care. Without an understanding of what may be taking place for them internally, it can become very difficult to empathise and adjust our behaviour accordingly.

Learning and behaviour are very closely linked, as learning how to behave in a helpful way is a learning process much like any other learning process. And we are certainly a long way from understanding the intricacies of exactly how the brain works in terms of learning and behaviour. However, research in neuroscience is increasingly providing new methods for understanding ways in which the brain learns, and this naturally aids our understanding of how behaviour develops.

THE EVOLUTION OF THE HUMAN BRAIN

The brain has three 'layers' – each one having developed at different points in human evolution. The oldest 'brain' is the **Reptilian brain**, and it governs the body's vital functions, such as heart rate, breathing, body temperature, and balance, as well as our most basic survival instincts. The **Limbic brain** emerged next in mammals. It is able to process and remember more complex behaviours, and it is responsible for what we call emotions in human beings. It is often reported to be the seat of many judgments that we often make unconsciously, and it has a strong influence on our behaviour. The **Neocortex** developed in primates and enabled, or supported, the development of human language, abstract thought, imagination, and consciousness.

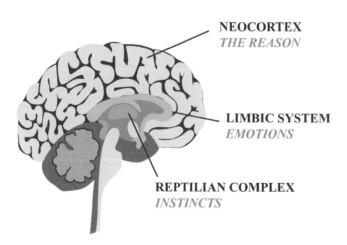

Figure 1.2 Layers of the human brain

HOW DOES THIS RELATE TO CHALLENGING BEHAVIOUR?

We know from an evolutionary perspective that certain events and situations increase stress hormones in the brain, triggering a 'fear' response. The Reptilian brain, as the oldest brain system, has always had a role in keeping us safe – it activates processes often referred to as **fight or flight** when danger is detected in the environment, prompting the body to do something to keep us safe. The events and situations triggering a 'fear' response will vary from person to person and from one situation to another. What one person finds threatening in the environment, another person may not. The reasons for this variation are many and varied. But often it boils down to whether the person feels able to **cope** with the situation they are faced with. As a means of keeping us safe, stress hormones make us threat-focussed – preparing the body to protect itself by either fighting, flighting (running), or freezing.

These 'threats' are not, however, always physical. If we think about this from an evolutionary perspective, one key purpose for the development of this system in the brain was to keep us, humans, safe from other animals and predators (e.g. the sabre-tooth tiger in Figure 1.3).

This response system developed primarily to ensure that if something in the environment (the tiger) posed a threat to our physical safety, our body could react quickly enough to keep us safe from harm. The way that we react would be to prepare to fight, prepare for flight, or freeze – with each response serving to keep us safe in response to different threats. In the Figure 1.3 example, although it is over-simplified, we can see that this safety system within the brain has been evolutionarily

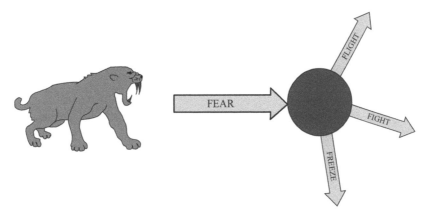

Figure 1.3 Threats and fear responses in prehistoric human life

beneficial and essential to humans throughout history. So we have always needed this system.

However, although the physical threats posed by predators occur less frequently within developed society, that safety mechanism in the brain still exists, as do situations that threaten people in other ways. That safety mechanism will be triggered by, and respond to, other non-physical threats within our environment. Many things with which we feel we **can't cope** or from which we feel a need to **protect ourselves** will trigger those same chemical responses that the sabre-tooth tiger did for our ancestors. What these 'triggers' are depends on many things, including the skills, abilities, and experiences of individuals, and there will be much variability from one young person to another.

Some young people will have very well-developed coping mechanisms and strategies when faced with a wide range of new and potentially threatening situations. Other young people, perhaps due to lack of experience, under-developed problem-solving skills, or other factors, may encounter numerous situations in everyday life, including school, which make them feel threatened. Regardless of what the threat is, as we have seen, the biological response to threat and fear is the release of chemical hormones in the brain to trigger the fight/flight/freeze response.

Very often, particularly in classroom situations, a young person who is fighting, flighting, or freezing can be very challenging for the teachers and adults trying to support them because these behavioural responses are not conducive to good order. And this is what we describe as 'challenging behaviour' or 'unwanted behaviour'.

So, one way to try to understand challenging behaviour is to frame it as the result of a person's fight/flight/freeze instincts being triggered. Regardless of how challenging

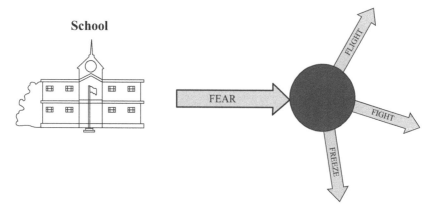

Figure 1.4 Threats and fear responses in modern human life

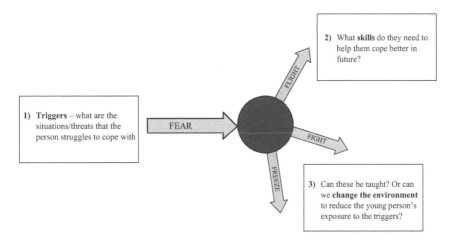

1) **Triggers** – what are the situations/threats that the person struggles to cope with

FEAR

2) What **skills** do they need to help them cope better in future?

3) Can these be taught? Or can we **change the environment** to reduce the young person's exposure to the triggers?

Figure 1.5 Threats and fear responses can emerge from many and varied triggers

a behaviour may be, if we are able to remember that something has triggered fight/ flight/freeze, then the next logical questions become: **'what triggered it?'** and **'what can I do to reduce that fear or that anxiety?'**.

The framework that we are going to explore provides starting points for developing our understandings of what the 'triggers' or 'fears' are for each young person we are supporting. This understanding is the foundation for developing a successful support plan for that young person, attempting to suggest ways that we can develop skills so that the young person is better able to cope with the situations they find threatening, and changing the environment and *our own behaviour* so that exposure to those threatening situations is minimised and coping skills gradually built up. If we are able to do this, we reduce the sense of threat, reduce anxiety, and reduce the activation of fight/flight/freeze.

UNDERSTANDING HOW TO UNDERSTAND CHALLENGING BEHAVIOUR

Example of how this 'threat detection' system might operate in schools

Gary is presented with a task by his teacher which requires lots of writing. Gary has been aware for some time that his writing is not as neat as the other children in his class, and that he makes lots of mistakes with his spelling. However, he has never told anybody about these feelings.

When the teacher begins to introduce the task to the class, Gary **feels threatened** – he thinks he might not be able to do this very well. He starts worrying that the teacher is going to criticise his spelling, and that his classmates are going to make fun of his writing. These **fears** of being laughed at quickly spiral and Gary feels very threatened by the situation (it is a threat to his self-esteem). His **safety instincts** kick in. He doesn't want people to laugh at his writing.

So, judging that people are going to be laughing at him very soon, and rather than attempt and fail at the writing, Gary begins making jokes about the names of his classmates. He likes it when he can make people laugh and thinks that telling jokes is something he is good at. His teacher tells him to stop, but Gary has noticed a few smiles in the room. Gary then makes another joke about somebody's name and starts singing this repeatedly. His teacher tells Gary to leave the room immediately, which he does. Once outside the room, with the threatening writing task out of sight, Gary begins to **relax**, having successfully **avoided** a situation where he felt likely to experience failure.

> **Threat (Fear) = damage to self-esteem**
> **Response (Safety Mechanism) = flight from the situation (avoidance)**

CAN WE CHANGE BEHAVIOUR?

Importantly, we also know that the brain can change, and we can learn new skills. This is because of what is called brain **plasticity**: the ability of the brain to acquire new information and to change because of this. One of the most crucial aspects to developing positive support for young people is identifying why the behaviour occurs, and then planning ways of teaching new, alternative, skills for the young person **to cope** and to meet their needs. It is to this end that we will now turn our attention.

> Brain plasticity means the ability of the nervous system to adapt continually to changing circumstances. This happens in everyone's brain whenever they learn something new – a new language, a new skill, a new route home, and even when they see a new face.
>
> (Blakemore & Frith, 2005, p. 123)

The strategies that we will explore in this book, and the many other strategies you will use in the course of supporting young people, effectively serve the purpose of minimising that fight/flight/freeze response by helping young people to cope better with the things they currently feel threatened by. In doing so, we are activating the Neocortex – the 'thinking' part of the brain – and developing automatic responses to situations which activate this part of the brain, rather than activating the Reptilian/Limbic brain systems.

WHY DOES CHALLENGING BEHAVIOUR HAPPEN? WHAT ARE THE THINGS THAT TRIGGER OUR FIGHT/FLIGHT/FREEZE RESPONSES?

The previous section summarised some of the biological processes which underpin the development of challenging behaviours by triggering the body's fight/flight/freeze responses. Because many of the unwanted behaviours we see in schools are driven by these chemical and developmental responses within the brain and body, behaviours can be quite resistant to change – the need to engage in that behaviour is often an automatic safety response.

The safety response (fight/flight/freeze) meets the need of keeping the young person safe. But safe from what?

The important information that we have to determine first and foremost is understanding what need is being met by engaging in that behaviour. This is not always an easy task, and the purpose of the behaviour may not be known even to the young person themselves. However, by being systematic in how we observe and reflect upon the behaviour, we should be able to make some helpful assumptions about why it is happening.

For example, does the young person present with unwanted behaviour because they are trying to:

* 'Flight' from a room that is too noisy, too bright?
* 'Fight' to let people know they are hungry, thirsty, or need the toilet?
* 'Freeze' to reduce confusion within the environment, including the social expectations?
* 'Freeze' to let us know that their work is too easy, boring, or too difficult?

It is also important to establish what predisposes this young person to needing to engage in the behaviour to meet this particular need:

- Are they suffering from a medical complaint or illness?
- Is there something lacking in their environment?
- Do they lack the communication skills to get this need met in other ways?
- Is this behaviour being inadvertently reinforced by people's responses to it?

NEED OR 'FUNCTION' OF BEHAVIOUR

Identifying which need, or **function**, is being met by the behaviour gives us a starting point for planning our support.

Whatever the reason for engaging in any behaviour, it can be categorised into one of the 5 functions listed in Figure 1.6.

Medical - are they in pain? always ensure that any possible medical reasons (hayfever, menstrual pain, dental pain etc) have been explored thoroughly

Tangible gain - is the young person trying to obtain something...a preferred object, toy, food? Are they trying to communicate a basic need like hunger?

Social change (attention) - is the young person trying to interact socially with other people? Is the young person trying to reduce social interaction?

Avoidance / Escape - is the young person using their behaviour to help them avoid or escape from a situation they find too difficult or a task that's too easy?

Sensory change - is the young person struggling to cope with the level of noise, heat, lighting or other sensory input?

Figure 1.6 5 functions of behaviour

AN ICEBERG OF CHALLENGING BEHAVIOUR

When thinking about the possible causes of challenging behaviours, the Iceberg Model (next page) provides us with a useful analogy to help shape our thoughts. A model of behaviour using the iceberg approach was used by Eric Schopler in his Parent Survival Manual (1995), and the principles here are very similar.

The Observable Behaviours are very often the focus point, and for very good reason! They are the symptom of the difficulty the pupil is experiencing, and it is our job as supporting adults to understand what that behaviour and those symptoms are telling us. Recording and documenting these surface behaviours is the easy part of any support process. The more challenging part is then thinking about why that behaviour is happening and what the pupil is communicating to us.

This understanding comes from diving below the surface of the iceberg. There are countless potential factors which make up the rest of the iceberg, and it is the weight of these factors that causes the iceberg to 'bob around' on the surface. And the better we get to know the person as an individual – their likes, their dislikes, their history – the better placed we will be to reach a useful understanding of their behaviour.

When we look at the iceberg, some of the factors below the surface are actually relatively easy to understand, if we are systematic in the way we approach our understanding of the situation. For example, there may be patterns of behaviour which we can observe – particular days of the week, particular times of day, particular lessons – which make it more likely that the behaviour will occur. Being aware of these patterns gives us very powerful information about what might be going on for the young person.

So, a young person whose behaviour deteriorates every time they are taught by Mr Lavan, often resulting in Mr Lavan being shouted at and sometimes having pens thrown at him, may not actually dislike Mr Lavan at all. However, the young person only comes into contact with Mr Lavan because he teaches English, and the young person has been struggling for a long time with basic skills in reading and writing. Just by making sure that we record the time and location of incidents, we can begin to very quickly understand some of those reasons behind unwanted behaviour that lie just beneath the surface of our iceberg.

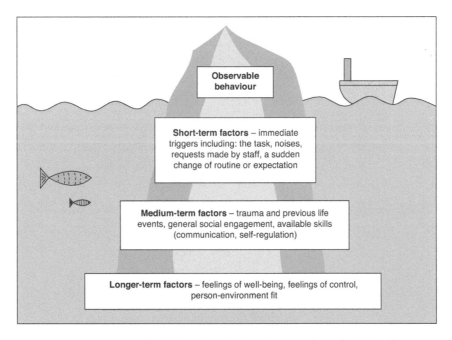

Figure 1.7 An Iceberg Model of challenging behaviour and underlying factors

5 REASONS CHALLENGING BEHAVIOUR OCCURS

In order to help a young person to change a behaviour or a set of behaviours, we need to have a clear understanding of **why the behaviour occurs** in the first place. What function does it serve for the young person? How can we help them to behave differently to achieve the same outcome next time?

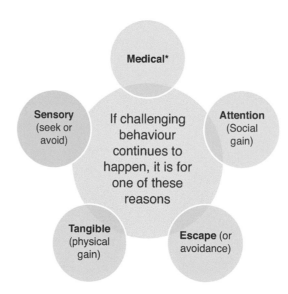

Figure 1.8 5 functions of challenging behaviour

*Always ensure that medical causes have been explored fully

SUMMARY OF CHAPTER I

In this first chapter we have begun the process of becoming more systematic in how we approach challenging behaviour. Thinking more deeply about **why behaviour occurs** is the first and most crucial part of becoming more systematic in our support. Incidents of challenging behaviour cannot be viewed as random, out-of-the-blue events that arise 'from nowhere'. They very rarely, if ever, are.

We have seen that evolutionary perspectives and biological factors can explain many key drivers for challenging behaviour and that there can be numerous influences lurking 'beneath the surface' of our iceberg.

Behaviour always occurs for a reason, to fulfil a purpose, and unwanted behaviour is exactly the same.

Understanding why behaviour is happening and what to do – using the flowchart

So we have begun our primary job as supporting adults: starting to understand **why that behaviour is happening** for a young person. We have looked at the five main reasons why challenging behaviour occurs; in addition, **the flowchart** presented at the end of this chapter (in Figure 1.10) offers a systematic way to try to analyse incidents in a structured way. Using the flowchart as one starting point, we can embark on the next stage of the helping process and begin to explore possible ways that we may wish to intervene.

In the remaining chapters we will explore further some of these suggested strategies. We will also explore the key things to consider when using the information we have about why behaviour occurs to help us plan to change things for the better in future, and to develop ways for the young person to **cope better** with the things that currently challenge them. All of this knowledge and planning will be pulled together into a **Coping Plan** – a 1-page summary of the young person's behaviour and the plans and strategies agreed upon by the supporting adults.

Figure 1.9 Process of assess-plan-do-review

Assess, plan, do, and review

The process of behaviour change is a complicated one, but our approach to helping doesn't need to be complicated. In fact, the simpler we can keep our approach, the easier it will be to help the young person towards positive change, and the less demanding it will feel for you as staff. For that reason, the framework we are going to use throughout the rest of this book – **The Coping Plan** – seeks to simplify what

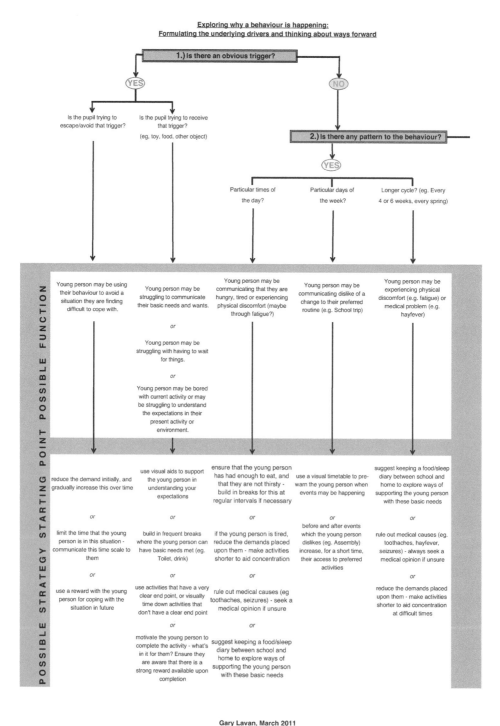

Figure 1.10 Flowchart for formulating the problem and solutions

we, as staff, do in response to challenging behaviour and to summarise all of our strategies on 1 page.

One of the core principles of the framework we are going to use is following a process: **assess-plan-do-review**. Chapter 1 has walked us through the vital first step in the helping stage: understanding the reasons for the behaviour. This is the first time we '*assess*' what is going on. Next, we want to turn that understanding into practical strategies ('*plan*') and actions ('*do*') that are going to be supportive for staff and helpful for the young person we are working with. In the following chapters we are going to explore what teachers and school staff can do to help at different phases of behaviour, starting with what helps keep the young person calm, what we do when challenging behaviour arises, and how we '*review*' what we are doing to make sure it is working.

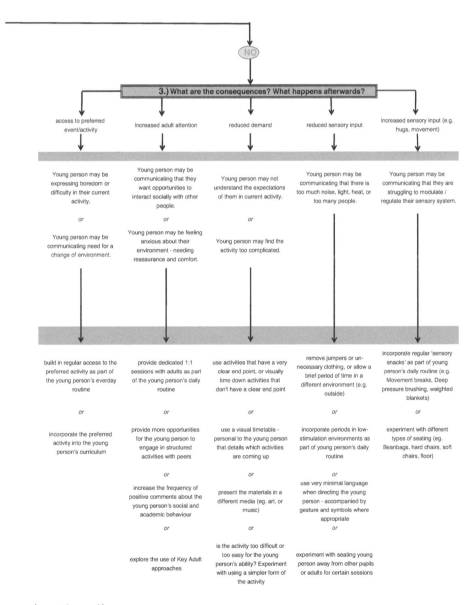

Figure 1.10 (continued)

CHAPTER I   REFERENCES

Blakemore, S., & Frith, U. (2005). *The learning brain: Lessons for education.* Oxford: Blackwell Publishing.

Department of Health (2009). *Valuing people now: A new strategy for people with learning disabilities.* London: TSO.

Emerson, E. (1995). cited in Emerson, E. (2001, 2nd edition). *Challenging behaviour: Analysis and intervention in people with learning disabilities.* Cambridge: Cambridge University Press.

Schopler, E. (1995). *Parent survival manual.* New York: New York Press.

CHAPTER 2
PLANNING FOR CHANGE

In the first chapter, we have examined the reasons **why** unwanted behaviour happens and looked at ways of identifying these reasons, using our flowchart as a starting point.

Once you have a good understanding of *why* the behaviour occurs, you need to begin planning how to help the young person to change the behaviour. This chapter begins to explore this next key question: **What can teachers and school staff do to help?** In answering this question and beginning to plan for positive change, we will develop a plan which will consider the following areas:

- Making changes to the young person's environment
- Teaching the young person the skills to meet their needs
- The motivators that are to be put in place to reinforce alternative positive behaviours
- How the unwanted behaviour will be managed when it occurs

In this chapter, we will introduce the main tool of the book: a 1-page template (the **Coping Plan**) that will be used to structure the following chapters. The Coping Plan is a document that breaks behaviour down into 4 phases, each having its own plan of action for staff to follow. The Coping Plan can be used as a tool by you as staff to capture the plans you make – so that all staff can see at a glance what strategies have been agreed and when to use them.

This is a crucial step in planning any support for pupils presenting with unwanted behaviour in school. Having a written plan of **agreement between staff** for how we respond to challenging behaviour is essential to ensure that we are consistent in our approach. We will discuss '**consistency**' in more detail later as it is the cornerstone of successful support for many of the young people we work with.

Before we dive into using the Coping Plan, it is helpful to continue a little further along our journey towards understanding more about challenging behaviour. The next section is going to walk us through another key concept.

That is, as well as always having a reason, all behavioural 'episodes', 'meltdowns', or 'incidents' **always follow a pattern**. And although it may not seem like it at the time, when emotions are high and the adrenalin is flowing, it is vital that we take time to reflect on the behaviour we are presented with and to become systematic in how we interpret and understand it.

2

We cannot provide effective support for challenging behaviour if we are always reacting to it. We must be systematic in our approach and proactive in our planning.

THE CHALLENGING BEHAVIOUR CYCLE

The first step to being consistent, systematic, and proactive is taken by understanding that all behaviour happens for a reason, as outlined in Chapter 1. The second step towards effective support comes from understanding that all behavioural episodes pass through the same cycle. The graph on the next page illustrates what this cycle typically looks like.

Clearly, not all incidents will pass through this cycle at the same speed. Some incidents will appear to happen very quickly, with a young person seemingly moving very rapidly from being calm and settled to being aggressive, disruptive, or non-compliant. Other incidents will be much more noticeable in terms of how the behaviour builds and escalates gradually, culminating in a display of unwanted behaviour, before calm and order is restored.

It is possible, however, to break down all episodes of challenging behaviour into the 4 'phases' in Table 2.1 which depict **what the young person is doing**.

It is essential to become aware of, and familiarise yourself with, the cycle we have outlined here. As stated already, all episodes of challenging behaviour will pass

Table 2.1 4 phases of the Challenging Behaviour Cycle

Phase 1	This is called the 'PROACTIVE PHASE'	All is calm. The young person is mostly relaxed and settled and engaging in their usual manner.
Phase 2	This is called the 'ACTIVE PHASE'	The young person's arousal increases; small changes in behaviour may be noticed. The young person may be described as starting to 'bubble'.
Phase 3	This is called the 'REACTIVE PHASE'	The point where the most significant challenging behaviour occurs and peaks.
Phase 4	This is called the 'RECOVERY PHASE'	After challenging behaviour has peaked and the young person begins to relax and calm, they may become upset, tearful, or remorseful.

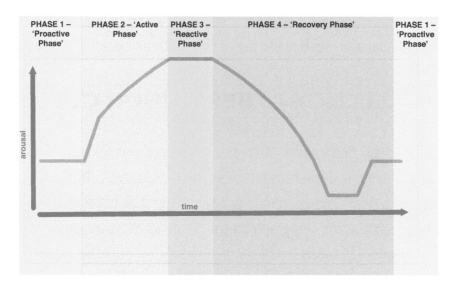

Figure 2.1 Challenging Behaviour Cycle – the Arousal Curve

through this cycle, and the young people we are working with may find themselves stuck in recurring cycles of behaviour if we are not able to analyse the cycle and find the crucial points at which to intervene.

The phases have been coloured as they are intentionally – to serve as memory aids as to **what staff should be doing** at these points in the cycle – in Table 2.2.

Table 2.2 4 colors of responding to the Challenging Behaviour Cycle

Phase 1	This is called the 'PROACTIVE PHASE'	YELLOW	Yellow = '**Mellow Yellow**' Here we are using strategies which we know help keep the young person 'mellow'.
Phase 2	This is called the 'ACTIVE PHASE'	GREEN	Green = '**Go**' Behaviour is beginning to escalate, and staff need to 'Go' – something needs to be changed; action must be taken.
Phase 3	This is called the 'REACTIVE PHASE'	RED	Red = '**Danger**' At this stage, proactive strategies have not been effective. The priority is reducing danger of harm and restoring order.
Phase 4	This is called the 'RECOVERY PHASE'	BLUE	Blue = '**Feeling Blue**' Actively difficult behaviour may be replaced by lower mood, upset, remorse. Strategies to help restore positivity are needed here.

THE COPING PLAN

So far we have undertaken assessment of the reasons why behaviour happens and started to break behaviour down into different phases. Hopefully this has already started moving us closer to developing effective strategies in response to the behaviour. In order to continue this journey, we can pull all of that assess-plan-do-review process together into a brief, 1-page summary document that is person centred and provides the basis for a consistent approach. On the next few pages, we will explore this summary document: the **Coping Plan**.

Take some time to familiarise yourself with it – we will be using this to organise all of our thinking and planning as we work through the approach together. Trying to understand and plan for very challenging behaviour can seem like a daunting task, and often it's exceptionally difficult to know where to begin with so much going on.

The Coping Plan helps us overcome this seemingly daunting task by breaking down the behaviour into the four distinct phases (Yellow, Green, Red, and Blue) that we have just explored. We know from experience and from psychological research that all challenging behaviour progresses through these four phases. Sometimes that happens very quickly, and sometimes it can be a slower journey, but once you are used to breaking the behaviour down into the different phases, it becomes much easier to plan your strategies for positive change.

A note on the psychological theory underpinning the Coping Plan framework

The framework we are exploring in this book culminates in the Coping Plan – to pull together the various strands of support for young people with challenging behaviour. Frameworks such as this have been promoted within psychological research and literature as being the most effective way of providing effective positive behaviour support for people presenting with challenging behaviour. As such, the Coping Plan is a manifestation of well-documented and research-evidenced practice relating to the management of challenging behaviour and the promotion of positive behavioural support practices. It is beyond the scope of this book to cover this research-base and theory in any detail, but references are provided at the end of this chapter for those who wish to explore this further, and signposting is also provided in Chapter 7 for those interested in reading and understanding more about positive behaviour support and the research-bases for this resource.

Several researchers (LaVigna *et al.*, 2002; McIntosh *et al.*, 2010) have advocated the use of frameworks that draw upon multiple evidence-bases in order to support challenging behaviour effectively. In describing support for pupils with challenging behaviour, Jordan (2001) states that 'Challenging behaviour is best dealt with through the same processes of understanding, reducing stress, and teaching, that underpin all good practice in working with individuals with autism' (p. 170). With regard to this notion, the Coping Plan, as a framework, does not seek to advocate for the implementation of any particular evidence-based approaches. Rather the intention is that we will seek to develop a supportive framework to address the needs of the young people we are supporting.

In my professional work with schools and families, I draw on approaches grounded in Applied Behaviour Analysis. LaVigna & Willis (1995), applying the principles of Applied Behaviour Analysis, propose the following principles, understandings, and actions as being crucial to the process of developing support for people presenting challenging behaviour:

1. Develop an understanding of the person's **strengths** and **interests**

2. Identify and **describe the behaviours** observed

3. Understand the **function of the behaviour** – developing empathy

    • e.g. to gain control, to reduce anxiety, to protect self-esteem

4. Do something to **effect a change**

    • Changes to the **environment**

    • Teach new **skills**

    • **Reinforce** the positives

    • React to behaviour in a way that will **communicate** more helpful alternative options or behaviours

It is with an understanding of this type of systematic approach that we will now turn to exploring the Coping Plan. The intention of the Coping Plan is to take the essential aspects of what we think we know from the research and literature about effective and positive support and translate that into a simple framework for use in your school or setting.

A completed example of the Coping Plan is provided in Table 2.3, followed by a blank version of the Coping Plan in Table 2.4 for you to use with the young people you are working with.

Table 2.3 Sample completed Coping Plan

Pupil name:		Possible reasons for behaviour:		Plan number:	
Date of Birth:				Completed by:	
Year/Class:		New skills to be learnt:		Shared with parents/ carers on:	

What staff do:
- Provide personal visual timetable (Now & Next)
- Use visual timers for tasks with no clear end point
- Give 'high 5' for successful attempts
- Activity break every 30 minutes (job around school, or 5 minutes in library corner, provide time-out card to do so)

Agreed Staff Responses:
- Check understanding of task (thumbs up/thumbs down?)
- Support with completing task
- Offer toilet break / 'Time-out' card / Give a job around school

1) The YELLOW Phase

where a person is mostly calm and relaxed

- Smiles
- Doodles on paper
- Responds to questions first time

2) The GREEN Phase

where a person starts to become anxious. Quick action must be taken to avoid challenging behaviour

- Frowns
- Taps pens/pencils on table
- Rocks on chair
- Mutters under breath

Observable behaviours

3) The RED Phase

where significant challenging behaviour occurs

- Shouts loudly
- Shouts repeatedly
- Swipes/throws resources

Agreed Staff Responses:
- Remove other children from classroom/area
- Sit facing young person signing 'calm'
- Offer choice using 'Now/Next board'
- Provide 'time-out' card and direct to calm area/tent in class
- Physically support speedy transition to calm area and provide calming activity box with visual timer

4) The BLUE Phase

where a person starts to relax again

- Will cry
- Will say 'I'm happy now'
- Will ask for a hug

Agreed Staff Responses:
- Allow 5 minutes with calming activity box
- Redirect to visual timetable
- Support into scheduled activity

Table 2.4 Coping Plan

Pupil name:		Plan number:
Date of Birth:	Possible reasons for behaviour:	Completed by:
Year/Class:	New skills to be learnt:	Shared with parents/carers on:

What staff do:

• • • • •

1) The YELLOW Phase

where a person is mostly calm and relaxed

2) The GREEN Phase

where a person starts to become anxious. Quick action must be taken to avoid challenging behaviour

3) The RED Phase

where significant challenging behaviour occurs

4) The BLUE Phase

where a person starts to relax again

Agreed Staff Responses:

Observable behaviours

• • •   • • •   • • •   • • • • • • •

Agreed Staff Responses:

• • •   • • •

Agreed Staff Responses:

• • • • • •

COMPLETING THE COPING PLAN

One of the main purposes of using the Coping Plan is to reduce some of the confusion and chaos that can exist around challenging behaviour. To do that we have to be very purposeful in being systematic about how we describe and understand what is going on.

For this reason, the Coping Plan is best completed in a logical order, which will be mapped out throughout the rest of this book and summarised in the box 'Completing the Coping Plan'.

STEP 1: DESCRIBE OBSERVABLE BEHAVIOURS

Completing the Coping Plan

Step 1: Describe Observable Behaviours

Step 2: Build up a personal profile for the young person

Step 3: Explore and record suitable Proactive Strategies to be implemented at the Yellow Phase

Step 4: Explore and record suitable Focussed Support Strategies to be implemented at the Green Phase

Step 5: Explore and record suitable Reactive Strategies to be implemented at the Red Phase

Step 6: Explore and record suitable Reflective Practices to be implemented at the Blue Phase

---

The first section to complete on our Coping Plan is the central square – the descriptions of the young person's observable behaviour. Often, if we haven't taken the time to look at behaviour systematically, it can seem overwhelming because there can be so many behaviours presented that it is difficult to know where to begin.

Describing Observable Behaviours

Sometimes when supporting staff seek to understand challenging behaviours, it is the sheer number of behaviours described, and the apparent randomness with which they occur, that can generate confusion about how best to intervene and support.

For example, when asked the question

"What behaviours would I see if I were observing him in class?"

a typical response might be something like

"He will swear, hit other children, cry, throw things, laugh really loudly. Rock on his chair fast so that I'm worried he might fall. Shout things out or mutter under his breath. Sometimes he'll leave the room."

As a starting point, this response feels very daunting, and may invoke feelings of confusion, despair, and anxiety. However, if we begin to look at those behaviours systematically and take the time to think more deeply about when they happen, we can begin to make sense of what is really happening. The behaviours described above are very unlikely to be happening simultaneously. More likely is that the behaviours happen with some kind of pattern, similar to the **Challenging Behaviour Cycle** discussed previously.

The first step to complete when using the **Coping Plan** is to describe these Observable Behaviours systematically. When describing behaviour, it is important to be:

- Objective
- Specific

In doing so, we should aim to describe what actually happens: What would somebody see if they were standing back and simply observing? The example Coping Plan provides an indication of what we should be aiming for here. The descriptions of the behaviours are specific, they are objective (only describing what is happening, without implying reasons), and they are also short.

In the completed Coping Plan, the following behaviours have been listed

Behaviours in the Yellow Phase

- Smiles
- Doodles on paper
- Responds to questions first time

Behaviours in the Green Phase

- Frowns
- Taps pens/pencils on table
- Rocks on chair
- Mutters under breath

Behaviours in the Red Phase

- Shouts loudly
- Shouts repeatedly
- Swipes/throws resources

Behaviours in the Blue Phase

- Will cry
- Will say 'I'm happy now'
- Will ask for a hug

Summary of Observable Behaviours

So why does THIS behaviour happen for THIS young person?

We have described the behaviour which is of concern or is challenging to us.

We have started thinking about the individual characteristics of the young person.

Now we need to start considering the environmental influences – the possible fears or needs being communicated by this behaviour.

Let's go back to our **flowchart** (Figure 1.10 in Chapter 1) and explore some of the reasons why this behaviour might be happening.

List your ideas in a table like Table 2.5.

We are now ready to transfer these descriptions of behaviour into our Coping Plan – being careful to place behaviours within the phase where they actually occur. Once we have completed the process of describing each Observable Behaviour and writing it down within the phase that it is most often seen, it becomes almost immediately easier to understand why we are going to intervene differently at each different

Table 2.5 List of Observable Behaviours and their possible reasons

Observable Behaviour(s)	Possible Reason (Function)
Gary places both hands over his head and rests his head on the desk.	Gary is communicating that the task is too difficult or that he doesn't understand the instruction.

stage. This is the first step on our journey to understanding the behaviour and creating helpful responses and interventions.

STEP 2: BUILD UP A PERSONAL PROFILE FOR THE YOUNG PERSON

Completing the Coping Plan

Step 1: Describe Observable Behaviours

Step 2: Build up a personal profile for the young person

Step 3: Explore and record suitable Proactive Strategies to be implemented at the **Yellow Phase**

Step 4: Explore and record suitable Focussed Support Strategies to be implemented at the **Green Phase**

Step 5: Explore and record suitable Reactive Strategies to be implemented at the **Red Phase**

Step 6: Explore and record suitable Reflective Practices to be implemented at the **Blue Phase**

If we think back to our **Iceberg Model**, we will see that the visible bit of the iceberg, the bit above the surface, is the 'observable behaviour' that we have now described and, with the help of our Coping Plan, begun to understand by breaking it down into four separate phases.

This is the first step in planning for change. It is also, perhaps, the easiest step! What follows requires creativity to generate a plan for responding to those behaviours that is going to be sensitive to the needs of the young person and helpful in enabling them to cope better with difficult situations in future.

A personal profile of strengths and areas for assistance

There are very few strategies which we can confidently say are going to be helpful for all individuals we work with. All young people are individuals, with their own individual likes and dislikes, tolerance thresholds, and skill-sets. In order to build effective interventions and strategies to support anybody, we have to know that individual. It is helpful to stop at this point, having mapped out behaviours more systematically, and to ask ourselves:

- What are the young person's **strengths**?
- What do **we** think they might need help with?
- What do **they** think they might need help with?

Looking for exceptions – when does challenging behaviour not occur?

An important area within our assessment, which can be easily overlooked if we are not careful, is thinking about times when challenging behaviour does not occur. Doing so can provide us with vital information about the young person, their existing coping mechanisms, existing strengths, and existing interests – all of which can be harnessed to reduce anxiety and promote feelings of wellbeing and accomplishment. For example, if we identify that the young person doesn't ever present with challenging behaviour at certain times of day, or with a certain member of staff, or when engaged in art – all of these factors could indicate things that we should be utilising in planning our support. Record any thoughts or observations about when and why challenging behaviour doesn't occur in a list similar to Table 2.6.

Table 2.6 Looking for positive behaviours and possible factors

Observable Behaviour(s)	Environmental factors(Who/What/Where/When)
Gary removes his hands from his head, and begins working.	Mrs Help is sitting next to Gary and repeating task instructions face-to-face.

Health	Likes	Dislikes
• Gary has hayfever which causes much discomfort • •	• Gary enjoys time alone to read • Gary likes knowing what is happening next in his day • Gary enjoys pop music	• Gary dislikes his timetable changing • Gary dislikes other people touching him

Figure 2.2 Example of notes on likes, dislikes, and health

A personal profile of likes, dislikes, and health

It is vital that we are engaged in an ongoing process of understanding the individual and building up a profile of their:

• Likes – what brings them joy and happiness?

• Dislikes – what causes them distress or anxiety?

• Health issues

All of these things are going to equip us with essential knowledge that can help us to build effective support plans and interventions. Keep a summary of these things as a quick reference to help with your planning and formulating.

SUMMARY OF CHAPTER 2

Coping Plans – the importance of being consistent

'Consistency' is a term that is widely used when discussing behaviour management – and rightly so. It is one of the fundamental building blocks of successfully supporting young people who present with behaviour which challenges us. However, actually delivering 'consistent' practice is not straightforward. It is prone to many influences, some from the adults themselves, some from the young person, and some from the wider environment. Often, one of the biggest factors in reducing the consistency of our approach is that different staff will adopt different strategies to deal with similar situations, depending upon their interpretation of why the behaviour is happening.

One of the intentions of using a structured framework like the Coping Plan is that it becomes a written contract that all staff can adhere to. Each member of staff who supports the young person has a very simple bullet pointed set of 'instructions' for agreed-upon ways of responding to behaviours at each phase of the cycle.

Now that we have been introduced to the Coping Plan, and begun describing the behaviours which challenge us, we will turn our attention to the individual phases of the behaviour cycle and start putting together a plan of action. Chapter 3 will focus on the first phase of the Coping Plan, the "Yellow Phase".

This is the most crucial phase within any cycle of behaviour. It is within this phase that we are able to proactively teach new skills for the young person to use in managing their own behaviour, and it is also where we can proactively make effective changes within the environment so that the chances of challenging behaviour occurring can be minimised or removed. If we have a good understanding of the behaviour, and we can use this to plan effectively in a preventative way, we may be able to dramatically reduce the number of times we progress through the more challenging phases of the behaviour cycle and develop a range of strategies which are effective in helping the young person to learn to cope better with the things which are challenging them.

CHAPTER 2   REFERENCES

Jordan, R. (2001). *Autism with severe learning difficulties*. London: Souvenir Press.

LaVigna, G., & Willis, T. (1995). Challenging behavior: A model for breaking the barriers to social and community integration. *Positive Practices*, *1*(1), IABA, Los Angeles.

LaVigna, G.W., Christian, L., Liberman, R.P., Camacho, E., & Willis, T.J. (2002). Rehab rounds: Training professionals in use of positive methods for community integration of persons with developmental disabilities. *Psychiatric Services*, *53*(1), 16–18.

McIntosh, K., Filter, K.J., Bennett, J.L., Ryan, C., & Sugai, G. (2010). Principles of sustainable prevention: Designing scale-up of school-wide positive behavior support to promote durable systems. *Psychology in the Schools*, Using prevention science to address mental health issues in schools, *47*(1), 5–21.

CHAPTER 3

THE YELLOW PHASE / "THE PROACTIVE PHASE"

STEP 3: EXPLORE AND RECORD SUITABLE PROACTIVE STRATEGIES TO BE IMPLEMENTED AT THE YELLOW PHASE

Completing the Coping Plan

Step 1: Describe Observable Behaviours

Step 2: Build up a personal profile for the young person

Step 3: Explore and record suitable Proactive Strategies to be implemented at the Yellow Phase

Step 4: Explore and record suitable Focussed Support Strategies to be implemented at the **Green Phase**

Step 5: Explore and record suitable Reactive Strategies to be implemented at the **Red Phase**

Step 6: Explore and record suitable Reflective Practices to be implemented at the **Blue Phase**

Step 3 of completing the Coping Plan requires an exploration of factors which will promote helpful behaviour and the Proactive Strategies that staff can use to help keep the young person relaxed and ready for learning. Relating back to the flowchart in Chapter 1 (Figure 1.10), we will now explore some simple strategy ideas appropriate for this stage of the plan, with step-by-step directions for implementation and use.

PROACTIVE STRATEGIES – PREVENTING THE BUILD-UP OF STRESS

As discussed earlier, when we were looking at the Challenging Behaviour Cycle, the speed at which people will move through the different stages of a behaviour cycle can vary greatly.

Often, when talking to staff and parents about unwanted behaviour displayed by a young person, adults will describe a point where the young person 'explodes' or 'snaps', frequently over a seemingly trivial matter. At these times, it is common for the supporting adults to feel frustrated because there was no apparent build-up to the event and, therefore, nothing that could have been done. At these times, the bucket analogy can be very helpful.

3

One of the key principles here is that sometimes the behaviour which we see – the bit of the iceberg which is above the water – does not occur as the direct result of an immediate, or obvious, trigger in the environment. Sometimes, the behaviour which we see happens as the result of a gradual build-up over time of many smaller stressors – the factors in our iceberg below the water. If we can pay close attention to these factors, it is often possible to plan effective strategies that will minimise the chance of challenging behaviour occurring by reducing the levels of stress the young person is experiencing on a day-to-day basis.

THE BUCKET ANALOGY

All people have a threshold of tolerance for stress – let's imagine that the young person carries this stress around with them in a bucket. Let's also imagine that the young person we are supporting is experiencing lots of things in the environment which cause them stress, anxiety, or fear, and that all of these things get added into the bucket.

Throughout their day, the young person encounters numerous events which cause them a small amount of stress. Each event during the day adds a little bit more stress into the bucket.

The bucket has a limited capacity – it can only hold so much 'stress'. For some people the bucket is quite large and they can add lots of bits of stress into the bucket. For other people the bucket is much smaller, and they can add far fewer bits of stress before the bucket is full.

People carrying a small bucket will encounter, at some point, another small event that means the bucket becomes full. At this point, the bucket will overflow, and the stress within the bucket will be released – often as challenging behaviour.

Even people carrying a large bucket that rarely gets full may reach a point in the day where the bucket is just too heavy. At this point, although the bucket may not overflow in a dramatic way, they may need to put the bucket down and rest.

Figure 3.1 The bucket

PROACTIVE STRATEGIES FOR REDUCING 'STRESS'

The remaining pages in this chapter are devoted to a range of strategies and approaches that have been effective for other young people as ways to reduce stress in their day-to-day experiences and to keep them in the 'mellow yellow' zone within our framework.

There are, of course, other ways you may choose to collect the information you need to understand the young person's situation. And the strategies listed here are by no means intended to represent an exhaustive list of the things you may choose to implement. Each of these strategies is provided as a starting point, to provide some initial ideas for things you may wish to include within your Coping Plans. Also, it is highly likely that some of these strategies may be more suitable to be included in other phases for some individuals.

The Yellow Phase strategies covered are:

- Strategy #1 – Using Choice
- Strategy #2 – The Bucket List
- Strategy #3 – Emptying the Bucket – audit tool for school
- Strategy #4 – Emptying the Bucket – audit tool for free-time
- Strategy #5 – Rapport & Positive Relationships
- Strategy #6 – Minimising Communication Errors
- Strategy #7 – 'Doing' and 'Being' Strokes
- Strategy #8 – Reward Schedules
- Strategy #9 – Visual Timelines
- Strategy #10 – Planned Breaks
- Strategy #11 – Sensory Snacks

YELLOW PHASE – STRATEGY #1

Using choice

Perhaps one of the most important things we can provide for young people presenting with challenging behaviour is a choice.

Control dynamics

When a young person is presenting with challenging behaviour, we already know that they are communicating a difficulty to us – something they are struggling to cope with.

3

What that specific struggle is varies from one individual to another. However, very often there is a common theme which unites many of those difficulties. That theme is **power and control**. The young person is experiencing a lack of power over the situation they are in. The difficulty they are experiencing is that they do not feel in control. The challenging behaviour which is presented is often a final attempt to regain some control.

Everybody feels less anxious when they feel they are in control of things. And anxiety frequently rises when people feel out of control. As an individual's challenging behaviour often arises in response to similar triggers, or in similar situations, it also often follows similar patterns. In this way, the behaviour itself becomes reasonably predictable for the young person. Because it is a familiar pattern of behaviour and responses, the young person is better able to predict what will happen next, and being able to predict what will happen next makes the young person feel more in control and less anxious, stressed, or overwhelmed.

So, as supporting adults, an understanding that the young person's behaviour may be signalling the need to feel more in control is helpful when considering the reasons for any unwanted behaviour.

If we think that the unwanted behaviour is in any way communicating a feeling of being out of control, then offering choices can be an effective way of helping the young person to feel that they have more control over a situation and hopefully reduce the need for them to gain control in other, less helpful ways.

In our example above, if we increase the range of choice a young person can make throughout the day, we can increase their feelings of being in control and reduce the number of times their fight/flight/freeze responses will be activated. Being given choices in any situation makes us feel like we have more control, and this in turn

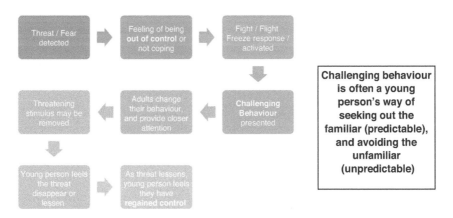

Figure 3.2 Simplifying the process of how challenging behaviour can serve to help people feel in control of situations

reduces our feelings of anxiety and of powerlessness. If we can reduce these negative feelings for the young people we are supporting, we can reduce the likelihood that the young person will need to use challenging behaviour to regain control over situations they are struggling to cope with.

Choice can be incorporated into the day-to-day experiences of young people in several ways:

Choice of activity

Can the young person be given options for some activities as to how they complete work?

- Using art, video, ICT, writing on paper, writing on the playground with chalk
- Choosing from a range of worksheets or books to use

Choice of location

Can the young person be given options as to where they complete certain activities?

- In class, at a table, on the floor, outside the classroom, on the playground

Choice of personnel

Can the young person be given options of whom they work with for activities?

- Work alone at workstation, work with one peer, join a group table, work with staff
- Lunch in the hall, lunch with staff in class, lunch with a peer in class

---

YELLOW PHASE – STRATEGY #2

3

The bucket list

As supporting adults, we have two things we must do:

1 Our first job is to try to build up a detailed picture of all the things throughout the day which will add bits of stress into the bucket that our young person is carrying. These things will be different for every person we work with. Once we are aware of these stressors, we can help to minimise the impact that they have on the young person by one of two means:

- Reducing how often we expose the young person to these events.

- Teaching new coping skills so that the young person is better able to tolerate them.

2 Secondly, we must try and build up a detailed picture of all the things that bring joy and happiness to the young person, so that we can effectively remove some of the stress that is being carried in the bucket.

- Providing more frequent access to enjoyable events will effectively remove some of the stress from the bucket, making it far less likely that the bucket will overflow or become too heavy.

The bucket list

This summary page can be used to capture the things which we know, or suspect to be, sources of stress for the young person. Simply add items to the bucket to keep a running record of things that we know can be difficult for the young person!

Young person name:	Date started:

My Bucket List

1. _____
2. _____
3. _____
4. _____
5. _____
6. _____
7. _____
8. _____

Figure 3.3

YELLOW PHASE – STRATEGY #3

Emptying the bucket – audit tool – school

Getting the child's perspective on **what makes school a good place** for them is really important. Often, they will tell you things you haven't thought of! Record their responses to capture the child's ideas – use drawing, writing, or any other medium – whichever works best.

Instructions

1. Use a different box for each response. The child can draw or write – or they may want you to do this for them.

2. Ask the child to '*have a think about the best day ever at school'*. Tell me why it was so good.

3. Ask the child to '*tell me about the best lesson ever'*. Why was it so good?

4. Ask the child '*who are the best people at school'*? Why?

5. After you have some responses in the boxes, try to prioritise the most important, and practical, responses in the last box at the bottom.

6. With other staff, have a think about how any of the ideas could be used or adapted as strategies as part of the Yellow Phase in the Coping Plan.

Table 3.1 Good school days look like . . .

What would it take to have more 'good school days'? • • •			

YELLOW PHASE – STRATEGY #4

3

Emptying the bucket – audit tool – free-time

Getting the child's perspective on **what makes free-time enjoyable** for them is also really important. Record their responses to capture the child's ideas – use drawing, writing, or any other medium – whichever works best.

Instructions

1. Use a different box for each response. The child can draw or write – or they may want you to do this for them.

2. Ask the child to '*have a think about the best day ever'.* Tell me why it was so good.

3. Ask the child to '*tell me about the best game you've ever played'*. Why was it so good?

4. Ask the child '*who are the best people in your life*?*'* Why?

5. After you have some responses in the boxes, try to prioritise the most important, and practical, responses in the last box at the bottom.

6. With other staff, have a think about how any of the ideas could be used or adapted as strategies as part of the Yellow Phase in the Coping Plan.

Table 3.2 Free-time looks like . . .

What would it take to have more enjoyable free-time? • • •			

YELLOW PHASE – STRATEGY #5

Rapport and positive relationships

Positive relationships form the bedrock of good behaviour support, and **communication** is the basis for the **relationships** we develop with the young people we are supporting. It is crucial that we work to develop an awareness of how we interact with the young person we are supporting, and consciously strive to develop an **interaction style** that fits with the young person's needs.

Different styles of interaction and communication

One way that our interaction style can be described, based on work by Diana Baumrind (1966; 1967), who explored the different types of parenting styles, is summarised below.

Typically, interaction styles are grouped into four quadrants: Authoritarian, Permissive-Indulgent, Permissive-Neglectful (Detached), and Authoritative. These are not necessarily fixed traits for any individual, and they are prone to variation depending on the situation we are in.

Being aware of how we are interacting is the first step to making successful accommodations for the young person.

Each of the interaction styles is summarised here. As stated, being aware of how we are interacting with a young person is crucial to building the effective relationships required to support them to develop positive coping strategies, and reduce their use of challenging behaviours. Most often, it is an **authoritative style** which proves most successful in providing the basis for an effective relationship.

DISCIPLINE		TEACHER INVOLVEMENT	
		LOW	HIGH
	WEAK	PERMISSIVE-NEGLECTFUL	PERMISSIVE-INDULGENT
	STRONG	AUTHORITARIAN	AUTHORITATIVE

Figure 3.4 Interaction styles

Adapted from Baumrind (1966)

Authoritarian

The adult is quick to jump on every little thing; may use a loud voice to get attention. Very demanding and expects pupils to follow the rules. Warmth is rare.

Benefits of an authoritarian style are that it can sometimes generate immediate short-term compliance.

The risks are that this type of interaction style can raise pupil anxiety and rarely produces long term changes in pupil behaviour over time.

Permissive-indulgent

The adult is warm and supportive but not good at setting consistent limits. Thus, irritating or disruptive behaviour may be ignored or handled with weak reprimands.

Benefits of a permissive-indulgent style are that pupils like warmth and support.

The risks are that the adult has a lack of control, which can increase the young person's anxiety and sense of confusion.

Permissive-neglectful

The adult is not providing sufficient boundaries or limits on behaviour and young people needing emotional support do not receive it. Young people do not receive the academic support they need.

Benefits for this interaction style are not evident.

The risks are that young people make poor academic progress and those who need emotional support do not get it because clear behavioural limits are not communicated.

Authoritative

The adult is positive, kind, and supportive. A young person feels respected, but they know this adult 'means business'.

Benefits of an authoritative style are that young people develop trust and respect, and behavioural responses to the adult are orderly.

YELLOW PHASE – STRATEGY #6

Minimising communication errors

Communication consists of verbal and non-verbal aspects. As such, communication is a complex endeavour and making errors in our communications is natural and common. Having awareness of how we interact and spotting errors we make within our interactions is difficult, but some key errors to look out for when adapting our interaction styles include those emerging from our emotions and those emerging from our words.

Errors stemming from our own emotions

When faced with challenging behaviour, emotions can run very high. As staff trying our best to support somebody whose behaviour is communicating a difficulty coping, we can feel a multitude of emotions, both positive and negative. There is a real danger that these emotions can become visible to the young person through our behaviour. Preventing this from happening is a difficult feat to achieve. The following two principles can help us to simplify the process of keeping control of our own behaviour and emotional responses:

- *All* **positive feelings** should be shared with the child;
- **Negative feelings** should not be shared with the child.

Errors stemming from our use of verbal communication

When a young person is in a state of crisis or meltdown, their ability to process the words we are using is often diminished, meaning that:

- **Words** will often have little or no impact at all;
- **Persuasion** usually doesn't work;
- **Shouting** doesn't work.

Thinking about our interaction style and consciously adapting it is a vital skill if we are going to provide the young person with a solid foundation from which they can learn new strategies to cope with the challenges they encounter day to day. A helpful strategy, explored on the next two pages, is to develop a range of 'doing strokes' and a range of 'being strokes' which can be incorporated into our daily interactions with the young person.

YELLOW PHASE **– STRATEGY #7**

Using 'doing' and 'being' strokes

Using 'strokes' is another way of thinking about the type of attention we give and receive – so another form of communication we have with other people. A 'stroke' is a stimulation that one person gives to another person. In infancy, these are more often literal physical strokes, and as we get older these are replaced by more symbolic forms of stroking, such as praise (positive stroke) or criticism (negative stroke).

We all have a basic need for attention, and people will often work very hard to receive attention, either positive or negative – the old adage that any attention is better than no attention at all. Receiving positive strokes is one of the experiences which contributes to the development of healthy emotions and trust and confidence in other people, and it is for this reason that it is useful to purposefully increase the number of positive strokes that we use with the young person we are supporting.

We have two powerful choices when communicating strokes to the young person. The first we call 'being' strokes. The second we call 'doing' strokes.

'Being' strokes

Being strokes are any positive comments we make about the young person, without them having to do anything at all to earn them. For example:
- 'It's good to see you'
- 'I'm looking forward to working with you tomorrow'

'Doing' strokes

Doing strokes are any positive comments we make about things the young person has done. For example:
- 'Thank you for having a go – you tried really hard'
- 'That's a really good choice you've made'
- 'I couldn't have done that without your help'

Making a conscious effort to increase the use of these strokes and to actively seek out opportunities to make positive comments is essential to the maintenance of positive relationships between staff and the young person.

YELLOW PHASE – STRATEGY #8

Reward schedules

Doing and being strokes, discussed in the previous section, are an easy way for staff to introduce additional positive interactions with the young person at various opportunities throughout the day and to acknowledge and reinforce appropriate, helpful, or desirable behaviours. For some young people, however, we might feel the need to introduce a higher level of positive interactions to try to draw attention to and reinforce positive and desirable behaviours that we think would be helpful for the young person to do more of. One way of introducing positive interactions in a more systematic and planned way is to develop a reward schedule, or a schedule of reinforcement.

Schedules of reinforcement have been used by psychologists for a long time, and have their roots in the behavioural psychology of B. F Skinner and C. B Ferster (1957). There are two types of reinforcement schedules to choose from:

1. Continuous reinforcement schedule

In practice, this type of schedule is very difficult to implement effectively. In a continuous reinforcement schedule, the desired behaviour is rewarded *every single time* it happens. For example, if we are trying to encourage a young person to remain seated when they are in class, they would receive a reward every time they sat down. Often, this level of rewarding is only used in the very first stages of learning the new behaviour, and then gradually reduced to an intermittent schedule.

2. Intermittent reinforcement schedule

In intermittent reinforcement, the helpful behaviour is rewarded only *some of the time*, and these schedules are therefore easier to implement within a busy classroom environment. We have four options when choosing an intermittent schedule:

a) **Fixed-ratio schedules**

   If we stick with our example of trying to encourage a young person to remain seated in class, to use a fixed-ratio schedule we would agree, as staff, that the young person will be given a sticker on their chart e.g. every 3rd time that they follow an instruction to sit in their seat.

b) Variable-ratio schedules

Again, thinking about the young person whom we are trying to encourage to remain seated in class: If we were to set up a variable-ratio schedule we, as staff, would agree that the young person will receive a sticker at varying times. For example, a sticker may be provided the first time they sit in their seat, but the next sticker will come the 4th time they do so, and then the 6th, 7th and 10th. Varying the schedule in this way means the young person isn't necessarily aware when they will receive a sticker, but they know that if they keep doing the new behaviour, they are going to get stickers at some point that lesson.

c) Fixed-interval schedules

To set up a fixed-interval schedule, we as staff would agree that the young person will receive a sticker after every, say, 10 minutes of having being seated in their seat. This would occur for every 10-minute interval that the young person is seated.

d) Variable-interval schedules

To set up a variable interval schedule, we as staff would agree that stickers will be provided at random time points while the young person remains seated. For example, the may receive a sticker after 1 minute of being seated, and the next sticker after 6 minutes, 8 minutes, 14 minutes, and 15 minutes. As with a variable-ratio schedule, the young person knows that if they continue sitting in their seat they will receive stickers but isn't sure when they will be provided.

YELLOW PHASE – STRATEGY #9

Visual timelines

When we talked about using choice earlier, we talked about young people having difficulty with unpredictability. Any strategies that we can employ which increase a young person's ability to predict what is going to happen that day, that week, that lesson, will help to ease any build-up of anxiety that they may otherwise experience.

Visual timelines can be very helpful for a young person who struggles with adapting to new or unfamiliar situations.

In **day-to-day** activities, visual timelines can be useful when the young person is:

- Going somewhere new
- Doing something new
- Following a different routine

Additionally, when used within **lesson tasks** or activities, visual timelines serve to let the young person:

- Know what they should do next in a task or activity
- Follow a task without adult support
- Reassure themselves that they are doing the task correctly

Visual timelines for session-to-session

For helping the young person understand daily routine and changes to their scheduled activities, a half-day, full-day, or full-week calendar can be used. Typically, this will show each major activity presented in sequence. Pictures or photographs are usually helpful to accompany the descriptive words used (see Figure 3.5).

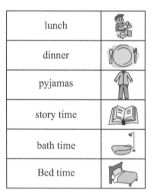

Figure 3.5 Sample visual timeline for home

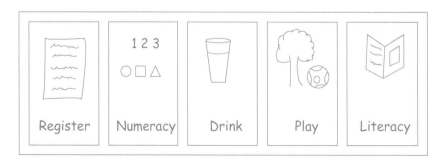

Figure 3.6 Sample visual timeline for school

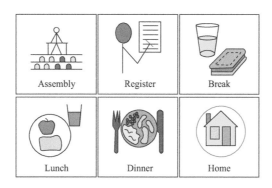

Figure 3.7 Sample visual timeline for full day

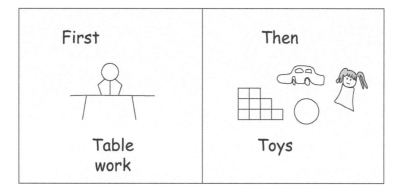

Figure 3.8a Sample First/Then timeline

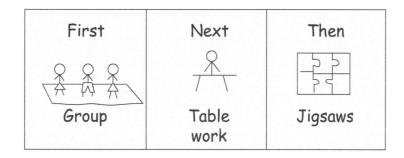

Figure 3.8b Sample First/Next/Then timeline

For some young people, the use of full-day or even half-day timelines can be a little too much information, and all that may be required is information regarding the next change or transition. In these circumstances, a Now/Next or First/Next timeline is often sufficient.

Visual timelines for within activities

Visual timelines can be used to help the young person understand task requirements and expectations and to help them work through tasks independently. These can use a similar format to the session-to-session timelines above, or they can be self-generated lists (1, 2, 3) that the young person creates at the start of each task. These can be generated on a wipeable board and re-created at the beginning of each task.

```
Gary's task board

1. date / title          ☐

2. 10 sums               ☐

3. colour in worksheet   ☐
```

Figure 3.9 Sample of a timeline used within an activity

Using visual timers

Visual timelines do an excellent job of communicating and clarifying the sequence of events, but for some young people the amount of time they are spending on an activity can prove to be a further source of anxiety or stress.

To help a young person cope with this demand, an additional strategy often used in conjunction with visual timelines is a visual timer. Often sand timers/egg timers will be used, but a range of timers, including clocks, stopwatches, and countdown timers on a whiteboard, can be effective in containing anxieties about *when* a change is coming up, as well as *what* the change will be.

YELLOW PHASE – STRATEGY #10

Planned breaks

Planned breaks can be a really powerful strategy for supporting many young people who present with challenging behaviour. This type of strategy links very closely with the analogy of 'The Bucket' discussed earlier. Essentially, the function of Planned Breaks is to build in to the young person's timetable and daily routines multiple opportunities to remove some of the stresses that have built up over that day or week. Planned breaks can take many different forms.

- For some young people, it will be most helpful to have regular opportunities for positive contact with key adults in school – **a check-in** at key points during each day to help the young person to maintain their focus on targets and objectives agreed at an earlier time.

- For others, it might be that access to Sensory Snacks (**targeted sensory input**) at regular points throughout the day will be helpful for them to relieve any build-up of stress caused by being overloaded by noise or other sensory factors.

- Other pupils may benefit from regular timetable access to motor activities and **movement breaks** to provide them with access to physical activity – rather than waiting until the young person seeks out this physical movement for themselves by wandering, running, or climbing.

Table 3.3 shows a sample timetable for Gary from *before* the introduction of planned breaks.

Table 3.3 Sample timetable for Gary *before* planned breaks

	MONDAY	TUESDAY	WEDNESDAY	THURSDAY	FRIDAY
Lesson 1	Literacy	Literacy	Literacy	Literacy	Literacy
Break	Free play	Free play	Free play	Free play	Free play
Lesson 2	Numeracy	Numeracy	Numeracy	Numeracy	Numeracy
Lesson 3	Numeracy	Geography	Religious Studies	PSHE	Design Technology
Lunch	Free play	Free play	Free play	Free play	Free play
Lesson 4	Science	French	P.E.	Science	History
Lesson 5	Art	Music	P.E.	Science	Project

Table 3.4 shows a sample timetable for Gary written *after* the introduction of planned breaks.

Table 3.4 Sample timetable for Gary *after* planned breaks implemented

	MONDAY	TUESDAY	WEDNESDAY	THURSDAY	FRIDAY
Planned Break	Check-in	Check-in	Check-in	Check-in	Check-in
Lesson 1	Literacy	Literacy	Literacy	Literacy	Literacy
Planned Break	Sensory Snack	Sensory Snack	Sensory Snack	Sensory Snack	Sensory Snack
Break	Free play	Free play	Free play	Free play	Free play
Lesson 2	Numeracy	Numeracy	Numeracy	Numeracy	Numeracy

	MONDAY	TUESDAY	WEDNESDAY	THURSDAY	FRIDAY
Planned Break	Relaxation	Relaxation	Relaxation	Relaxation	Relaxation
Lesson 3	Numeracy	Geography	Religious Studies	PSHE	Design Technology
Planned Break	Sensory Snack	Sensory Snack	Sensory Snack	Sensory Snack	Sensory Snack
Lunch	Free play	Free play	Free play	Free play	Free play
Lesson 4	Science	French	P.E.	Science	History
Planned Break	Relaxation	Relaxation	Relaxation	Relaxation	Relaxation
Lesson 5	Art	Music	P.E.	Science	Project
Planned Break	Reflection	Reflection	Reflection	Reflection	Reflection

YELLOW PHASE **– STRATEGY #11**

Using sensory snacks

Sensory Snacks is a term used to refer to Planned Breaks which have a focus on reducing or providing additional sensory input for young people. Not all young people will require this kind of approach, and the appropriateness of using Sensory Snacks relies upon staff developing a robust understanding of the young person and their individual needs – as described earlier when we discussed building up a profile for each young person we are working with.

If we look back on our flowchart (Figure 1.10) and our exploration of the five main reasons for challenging behaviour, we will see that 'sensory seeking' or 'sensory avoidance' was one of the main factors identified as a cause or trigger for challenging behaviour. Some young people with whom we work may well present with over- or under-sensitivity to things like:

- Noise
- Light

- Heat
- Smell
- Touch

If we are careful and systematic in our observations of when challenging behaviour occurs, it may well be the case that one or more of these factors seems to be present before some incidents. For example, it may be that challenging behaviour is noted to be more likely if the young person is in a session in the hall, rather than in the classroom. Part of our hypothesis, within our individual profile for that young person, may be that they struggle with noisy environments. Once we identify a need, or a reason for challenging behaviour such as this, we should plan to support the young person with that situation.

One option after having identified this factor could be to limit the young person's access to such environments or sessions. This would hopefully achieve the aim of eliminating the challenging behaviour from that situation – but how helpful is that going to be for the young person in the long run? After all, we can't guarantee that they will never encounter 'noisy' or 'busy' environments in the future. So, it may be that what we want to do is introduce some strategies to help them cope better with those situations, rather than teaching them to avoid them altogether.

In the example, here, where 'noise' or 'busy-ness' seems to be a trigger, and therefore something the young person struggles to cope with, it may be that we can help prepare the young person for such times by introducing sensory snacks – before, during, or after these problematic sessions take place.

Sensory snack example

Need/trigger identified = poor tolerance of 'noisy' or 'busy' environments

Challenging behaviour = young person frequently runs from the room and hides under desks in classrooms

Function of behaviour = escape/sensory avoidance

Suggested strategy =

- **before** any 'noisy/busy' sessions, the young person has access to 5 minutes of uninterrupted quiet time
- **during** any 'noisy/busy' session, the young person has access to an exit card which they can pass to staff to allow another 5 minutes of uninterrupted quiet time

---

- **after** any 'noisy/busy' session, the young person has access to 5 minutes of reflection time with a member of staff

The extent of these strategies will be determined by our prior knowledge of the young person and the individual profile we have built up – some young people may need a high level of support, such as that outlined above. Others may only need intervention at the **before** stage, or at the **during** stage, or at the **after** stage. There is no one-size-fits-all approach.

SUMMARY OF CHAPTER 3

The Yellow Phase / "The Proactive Phase"

Now that we have considered some of the aspects that will be helpful for keeping the young person relaxed and calm and developed some ideas for teaching the young person new coping strategies so that they can understand their emotions and better manage their behaviour, it's time to complete the Yellow Phase, the first section of your Coping Plan.

You may have found some of the strategies discussed useful and appropriate for the young person you are supporting, or you may have decided that some alternative approaches are going to be more helpful and appropriate.

In the completed example of the Coping Plan we looked at in Chapter 2, there were 4 identified strategies at this stage of the plan. See Figure 3.10 to review them.

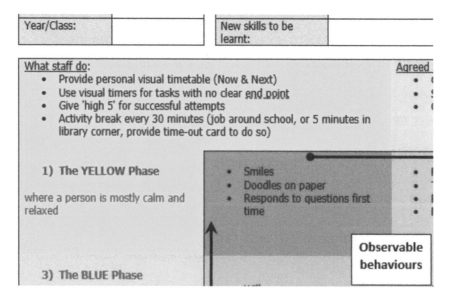

Figure 3.10 Yellow Phase of completed Coping Plan from our completed example in Chapter 2

CHAPTER 3   REFERENCES

3

Baumrind, D. (1966). Effects of authoritative parental control on child behavior. *Child Development, 37*(4), 887–907.

Baumrind, D. (1967). Child care practices anteceding three patterns of preschool behavior. *Genetic Psychology Monographs, 75*(1), 43–88.

Ferster, C.B., & Skinner, B.F. (1957). *Schedules of reinforcement.* New York: Appleton-Century-Crofts.

CHAPTER 4
THE GREEN PHASE / "THE ACTIVE PHASE"

STEP 4: EXPLORE AND RECORD SUITABLE FOCUSSED SUPPORT STRATEGIES TO BE IMPLEMENTED AT THE GREEN PHASE

Completing the Coping Plan

Step 1: Describe Observable Behaviours

Step 2: Build up a personal profile for the young person

Step 3: Explore and record suitable Proactive Strategies to be implemented at the Yellow Phase

Step 4: Explore and record suitable Focussed Support Strategies to be implemented at the Green Phase

Step 5: Explore and record suitable Reactive Strategies to be implemented at the Red Phase

Step 6: Explore and record suitable Reflective Practices to be implemented at the Blue Phase

Step 4 of completing the Coping Plan requires an exploration of what factors will help to de-escalate behaviour if it begins to deteriorate. We will introduce some strategies that staff can use to help the young person relax and calm. Relating back to the flowchart in Chapter 1 (Figure 1.10), we will explore some simple strategy ideas appropriate for this stage of the plan, with step-by-step directions for implementation and use.

Spotting patterns and analysing behaviour

We have talked about the importance of understanding exactly **why** a behaviour continues to happen. And you should now have some ideas about the types of strategy that might be helpful to use on a day-to-day basis to help the young person to cope better with the things they are finding difficult. Developing a plan to this stage is often a tricky task, as the reasons for unwanted behaviour can be difficult to unpick, and there can also be disagreement between supporting adults as to why a behaviour happens. An important role of the supporting adults is to be the detective, and to analyse the behaviour, looking for patterns and triggers that can serve as clues about why the behaviour happens, what function it serves, and what the behaviour is communicating for the young person. To develop a clear picture of the behaviour and to find the answers to these questions it is important to collect evidence in as systematic a way as possible. Behaviour record forms such as Frequency Charts, ABC charts, and detailed Incident Records are useful for this purpose. We will discuss the use of ABC forms and ABCC forms here and explore how they can help us understand the behaviour.

In continuing to develop our understanding of why the behaviour occurs, some of the things we need to know are:

- How often does the young person present with this behaviour?
- How intense is the behaviour?
- When does the behaviour present?
- Are there any obvious triggers for the behaviour?
- What happens for the young person afterwards?

For this reason, it is often not until we reach the **Green Phase** of the behaviour cycle that we can collect detailed information to develop our understanding of any patterns of behaviour that may exist. The Green Phase is also a crucial phase in the behaviour cycle for staff to intervene and make some changes to prevent behaviour escalating to a crisis point or meltdown. For this reason, we will explore here some strategies to hopefully help the young person to cope better and to deescalate their behaviour before it becomes challenging for us or unhelpful to them.

ACTIVE STRATEGIES FOR REDUCING 'STRESS'

The strategies listed here are by no means intended to represent an exhaustive list of the things you may choose to implement. Each of these strategies is provided as a starting point to provide some initial ideas for things you may wish to include within this stage of your Coping Plans. In the research and literature, models of support for challenging behaviour refer to strategies at this point in the cycle as Focussed Support Strategies (LaVigna & Willis, 2005). It is likely that some strategies identified here may also be suitable to be included in other phases, and that strategies covered elsewhere may be applicable at this stage of your plan.

The **Green Phase** strategies covered are:

- Strategy #1 – ABC Charts and ABCC Charts
- Strategy #2 – Antecedent Interventions
- Strategy #3 – The Grab-Bag

GREEN PHASE – STRATEGY #1

ABC charts and ABCC charts

A useful way of capturing and thinking about the information we have about the behaviour is to use a systematic approach such as ABC charts (see Table 4.1) or ABCC charts (see Table 4.2).

Two blank charts are provided on the following pages. The first is an example of an ABC chart. The second is an example of an ABCC chart. ABC charts help us to analyse the behaviour that we see and to think about it in a more systematic way. ABCC charts are just an extended version, with the additional task of forcing us to continue the process of understanding what a young person is trying to communicate through their behaviour.

Either form can be helpful, with the ABC offering a slightly simpler and slightly quicker tool to use, and the ABCC offering a more comprehensive analysis of the function of the behaviour – usefully completed with colleagues if this is possible. Whichever you choose is up to you, and will likely depend upon time factors and how confident you feel in being able to interpret the behaviours described.

Interpreting the evidence

Once we have collected the evidence, it is important to analyse it and interpret it. One of the most important things to do is to use the information together with your knowledge of the young person to come up with a hypothesis (an informed guess) as to what function this behaviour might have for this young person.

ABC and ABCC charts – what to do

1. Either select a time to carry out focussed observations, or take time after an incident to complete one of the forms.

2. Complete the columns on the chart as follows:

   • **Date and time** – these are very important pieces of information as they may highlight a pattern to the behaviour over time (e.g. unwanted behaviour occurring more frequently prior to sessions in the hall or unwanted behaviour occurring more frequently in the final 10 minutes of lessons).

- **A = Antecedent** – sometimes called the 'trigger'. What was happening just before the behaviour? Spotting the antecedent is a crucial clue as to what the young person is trying to communicate.

- **B = Behaviour** – In this column it is important that we just describe what we can see. Try to avoid phrases like 'became challenging' and instead state specifics, such as 'threw pens', 'shouted at peer', 'ran out of room'.

- **C = Consequence** – what happened for the child because of the behaviour? Again, be specific (e.g. did they get time with an adult, did they avoid completing a task).

- **C = Communication** – If you are using the ABCC chart there is an extra column for you to suggest what you think the child is trying to communicate through the behaviour described (e.g. 'When I leave the room I always get to talk to Mrs Staff'). It can be most helpful to complete this column as a whole staff team – and agree what you think the behaviour is communicating. Doing so will provide the basis for planning interventions and strategies that everybody agrees with.

Table 4.1 ABC chart – Antecedents/Behaviour/Consequences

Date	Time	A. Antecedents What was happening before the behaviour occurred?	B. Behaviour What did . . . . .do?	C. Consequences What you/others did after the behaviour occurred.

Table 4.2 ABCC chart – Antecedents/Behaviour/Consequences/Communication

Date	Time	A. Antecedents What was happening before the behaviour occurred?	B. Behaviour What did. . . . . .do?	C. Consequences What you/others did after the behaviour occurred.	C. Communication What is the behaviour communicating?

GREEN PHASE – STRATEGY #2

Antecedent interventions

This 'strategy' is actually a range of different strategies and approaches that can be used to hopefully change behaviour quickly by first changing something in the environment.

Often when a young person is in the Green Phase, staff will notice that their behaviour has changed. The young person may be described as 'bubbling' and they may be behaving in ways that let staff know that if something isn't changed, behaviour is likely to become challenging very quickly. The following strategies are different principles that staff can use to make changes to the environment quickly.

1. A high probability sequence

    This strategy requires the adult to build some momentum by encouraging the young person to comply with directions before giving the 'difficult' direction. For example, if a young person struggles to tidy resources/toys away after an activity, we call this a low probability task – there is a low probability they will do it. The adult:

    *   Builds up to requesting this by cultivating trust in compliance by asking the young person to do something we are fairly sure they will comply with (e.g. 'Give me a high five')

    *   And then ask something else they are likely to comply with (e.g. 'Jump in the air')

    *   And then gives the 'difficult' direction of 'Pens back in the box'

    The sequence starts with some low demand, fun tasks that have a high probability of compliance, which are quickly followed by the one task with a low probability of compliance.

2. Choice

    We have explored the power of offering choices in the Yellow Phase already. It is never too late within a behaviour cycle to offer choices to a young person, and doing so within the Green Phase may be sufficient to prevent behaviour from escalating further.

3. Introducing Motivating Situations

Sometimes we may need to introduce some motivating situations to encourage participation or compliance, and reduce the stress, anxiety, or fear the young person is experiencing. Having access to motivating toys, games, activities, locations, and people will be discussed in Strategy #3 – The Grab-Bag.

GREEN PHASE – STRATEGY #3

The Grab-Bag

The **Green Phase** of the behaviour cycle is where we begin to notice changes in behaviour. This is the most crucial time for staff to be able to intervene to make changes to the environment and reduce the likelihood of behaviour escalating to crisis point. When the young person's behaviour changes, they are communicating to us that something isn't right, that they are struggling to cope with something.

At these times it is often the case that staff know that something needs to change, but that there isn't always an easy way to do so. The 'Grab Bag' is one strategy that can be implemented and used quickly and effectively across a range of situations in school and out of school to make rapid changes to the environment and hopefully to the young person's feelings about their ability to cope with what is happening.

The 'Grab-Bag' is a rucksack or similar container that holds a variety of activities that are known to be calming and/or relaxing for the young person. For example, the Grab-Bag might contain:

- colouring activities
- jigsaws
- a football

The intention is to provide the young person with access to these activities in an effort to rapidly reduce the stress they are experiencing at any given time. Staff can signal to the young person that they can have 5-minutes time out, grab the bag, and provide the young person with a choice of the activities inside.

Challenging behaviour often serves the function of helping people to feel more in control of their environment, and better able to predict what is going to happen next. A known pattern of challenging behaviour and predictable responses from adults is often less stress-inducing than a lesson or situation where the young person can't predict what will happen next and can't control whether they will be asked to do things they find difficult.

So one way we can help is to provide the young person with alternative behaviours/activities to engage in which we know they also enjoy, are familiar with, can predict, and therefore help them to feel back in control of events – removing some of the stressors that may have filled up the 'bucket' that day.

Grab-Bag example

Staff have undertaken a detailed assessment of all of the things that Gary enjoys both at home and at school. Through this assessment, a number of activities have been identified which Gary has at one time or another sought as a means to successfully calm himself when he has felt overwhelmed. Staff also identified a number of situations which often caused Gary to feel overwhelmed.

Figure 4.1 The Grab-Bag

The **activities/experiences** identified were:	The **overwhelming situations** identified were:
• Completing 10-piece jigsaw puzzles • Completing dot-to-dot puzzles • Listening to music	• Being in noisy rooms • Being in large open spaces • School assemblies

Staff decided that they were going to make available a small rucksack containing:

- 2 favourite jigsaws;
- a book of dot-to-dot puzzles;
- an iPod with favourite music tracks

This was taken by staff working with Gary for all sessions that took place outside of the classroom. It was taken to school assemblies, to the dinner hall, to PE lessons, outside at break times, and on any off-site trips.

Whenever Gary started to feel overwhelmed in school, staff knew that he began playing with his sleeves and collar and would often begin rocking from side to side. The new strategy was now that whenever staff noticed these pre-cursor behaviours, staff would pick up the Grab-Bag, and Gary was asked to go with a member of staff to a quieter space nearby. Gary was given a choice of activities from the bag, and staff used a five-minute sand timer to let Gary know how long he would be able to use the chosen item before returning to the original session. Staff were now able to use a consistent approach to reduce the number of times Gary's behaviour escalated to the point where it became very challenging for staff.

Grab-Bag – some considerations

Q. What if the young person uses challenging behaviour more often so that they can get access to the activities in the bag?

There is a danger with any strategy that involves the provision of preferred activities that the young person will establish a link between their challenging behaviour and gaining access to the things they like. To guard against this, it is important that we do two things:

1. We implement the strategy as soon as we notice the pre-cursor behaviours – so that any link to obtaining the preferred activities is linked to lower level, pre-cursor behaviours, and not more extreme challenging behaviours.

2. We must make sure that these activities are provided at other times so that the young person is able to obtain them for positive or more desirable behaviour – in this way there is no link to challenging behaviour resulting in access to these things.

Q. What if they don't appear calm after their allotted 5 minutes?

The amount of time required will vary for each person and from situation to situation. Staff will use their best judgement to decide when it is right to return the young person to their timetabled activity. We can ease this process by helping the young person prepare for the transition back to the original activity using visual timelines, visual timers, talking the transition through, using 'doing' strokes, 'being' strokes, and other positive communications and interactions.

Q. What if we don't know what activities to use in the bag?

There are numerous activities which have a fairly universal calming effect for lots of people. These activities are always repetitive, don't have natural end points (i.e. they can be continued for long periods) and require a sustained focus and attention. If you are unsure what activities to use, these are good examples of easy-to-implement activities that often have naturally calming influences: drawing, colouring, playing with play-dough or plasticine, and using things like Hama beads, peg boards, and building bricks.

Grab-Bag development sheet

4

This page can be photocopied and used to help you plan what your Grab-Bag will look like.

Step 1 is to summarise what you know, from your assessment of the behaviour to date and from your experience of the young person's interests and likes:

Activities/experiences known to calm/relax:	Situations known to be **triggers** for the young person:
• • • • • • •	• • • • • • • •

Step 2 is to decide which of the calming activities/experiences will be practical to implement in your setting. For example, is it practical to have a football as one of the available activities? If so, then great. If not, is there a similar alternative that would work? You can list the suggested activities in the bag in Figure 4.2.

Figure 4.2 Grab-Bag activities

SUMMARY OF CHAPTER 4

The Green Phase / "The Active Phase"

In this chapter we have continued with our exploration of developing new strategies for reducing the likelihood of challenging behaviour occurring, and specifically considered some of the aspects that will be helpful for intervening when behaviour begins to escalate. Many of the approaches used here are described in the literature as antecedent interventions (Royal College of Psychiatrists *et al.*, 2007). With these Focussed Support Strategies in mind, it's time to complete the Green Phase, the second section of your Coping Plan.

You may have found some of the strategies discussed useful and appropriate for the young person you are supporting, or you may have decided that some alternative approaches are going to be more helpful and appropriate.

In the completed example of the Coping Plan we looked at in Chapter 2, there were 3 identified strategies at this stage of the plan. See Figure 4.3 to review them.

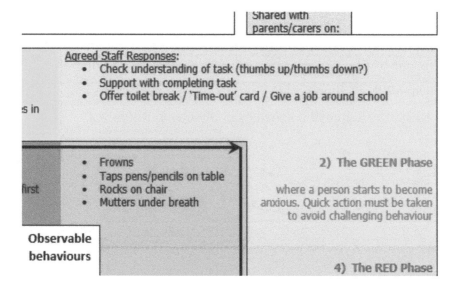

Figure 4.3 Green Phase of the Coping Plan from our completed example in Chapter 2

CHAPTER 4   REFERENCES

LaVigna, G., & Willis, T. (2005). Multi element model for breaking the barriers to social and community integration. *Tizard Learning Disability Review, 10*(2), 16–23.

Royal College of Psychiatrists, British Psychological Society, & Royal College of Speech and Language Therapists (2007). *Challenging behaviour: A unified approach.* London: Royal College of Psychiatrists.

CHAPTER 5

THE RED PHASE / "THE REACTIVE PHASE"

STEP 5: EXPLORE AND RECORD SUITABLE REACTIVE STRATEGIES TO BE USED AT THE RED PHASE

Completing the Coping Plan

Step 1: Describe Observable Behaviours

Step 2: Build up a personal profile for the young person

Step 3: Explore and record suitable Proactive Strategies to be implemented at the Yellow Phase

Step 4: Explore and record suitable Focussed Support Strategies to be implemented at the Green Phase

Step 5: Explore and record suitable Reactive Strategies to be implemented at the Red Phase

Step 6: Explore and record suitable Reflective Practices to be implemented at the Blue Phase

Step 5 of completing the Coping Plan requires an exploration of what factors will help to restore order quickly and keep everybody safe if behaviour becomes dangerous. We will explore some strategies and principles that staff can use to help the young person work through their emotions and feelings without hurting themselves or others.

Restoring order and going back to the drawing board

Essentially, if we reach this stage of the cycle, our only priorities are:

- Ensuring the safety of everybody involved.
- Reducing the intensity of the situation quickly.
- Restoring order.

Unfortunately, at this stage of the Challenging Behaviour Cycle, the situation has escalated to peak levels, and our overriding priority is de-escalation. Any strategies that we employ at this stage of the cycle are not intended to help the young person to learn any new skills or coping strategies. That is the job of the strategies we have in place at the Yellow Phase and the Green Phase. The strategies we use here should be non-aversive, and should have the sole intention of restoring order safely.

The key piece of learning for staff at these times is that the strategies and plans in place haven't worked on this occasion to help the young person to cope with the things they are struggling with. When reflecting after incidents have reached peak levels, staff should always remember that no plan can be faultless, and staff should support each other and remind each other of the successes and improvements that will have occurred over time in supporting the young person. However, there will be lessons that we can take away from each incident to hopefully inform our future plans and help us to incorporate new strategies or new approaches in the future.

In the research and literature, models of support for challenging behaviour refer to strategies at this point in the cycle as Reactive Strategies (LaVigna & Willis, 2005). The following pages will outline some principles for restoring order quickly and safely. However, the nature of adult intervention at this stage is going to be unique to each young person we are supporting and to each situation or crisis.

The **Red Phase** strategies covered are:

- Strategy #1 – De-escalation
- Strategy #2 – Diffusion
- Strategy #3 – Using Choice
- Strategy #4 – Counter-intuitive Strategies

RED PHASE – STRATEGY #1

De-escalation

Below are some guiding principles to support the effective de-escalation of challenging behaviour, particularly aggressive or violent behaviour. Specific strategies will need to be developed depending on the situation and your knowledge of the young person.

Generally unhelpful strategies

- Becoming visibly angry yourself, shouting, or raising your voice
- Not listening – i.e. trying to command the young person
  - e.g. 'Sit down and shut up now!'
- Confusing the young person by making too many demands
- Making sudden movements that could startle the young person or make them feel threatened

- Crowding the young person
- Using threatening body language

Generally helpful strategies

- Consider your own safety first (position yourself near the door if possible)
- Try to reduce young person's arousal level by:
    - Removing any other young people from the environment immediately
    - Turning off any sources of noise (radio, TV, etc.)
    - Lowering your voice
    - Talking in a calm and even tone
- Maintain appropriate eye contact at all times
- Change your body language to make it less threatening
    - Encourage the young person to sit down, then sit down yourself
    - Maintain a relaxed body posture and project calm

RED PHASE – STRATEGY #2

Diffusion

As with strategies for de-escalation, diffusion techniques are going to vary greatly depending on the situation and your knowledge of the individual. The following principles will be helpful in many situations.

Generally helpful strategies

- Contain the situation:
    - Allow appropriate venting if this is not causing physical harm, but let the young person know if it is getting too much
- Direct the young person clearly and confidently:
    - 'Gary, I need you to put the box down and sit down.'
    - 'It would be best to sit down and then we can talk about what's upsetting you.'
- Empathise with the young person and make them feel listened to and understood:
    - 'I can understand why that must be very hard for you.'
    - 'It sounds like Gary's really upset you.'

RED PHASE – STRATEGY #3

5

Using choice

During our exploration of the Yellow Phase we explored the use of choice as a strategy to increase feelings of being in control. The intention then was to increase the amount of choice throughout the day, to alleviate any build-up of stress, and to remove some of the stressors from the 'bucket'.

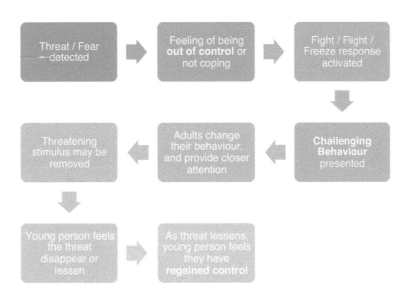

Figure 5.1 Figure simplifying the process of how challenging behaviour can serve to help people feel in control of situations

However, there may still be times when, despite our best efforts to create a positive and non-threatening environment, the young person still experiences stressful situations with which they struggle to cope. At these times, we can again turn to 'choice' as a viable and relatively easy strategy to employ.

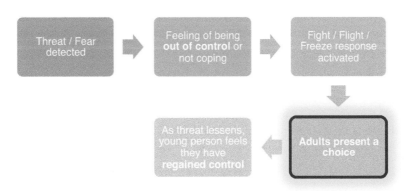

Figure 5.2 If we intervene at the right time, by offering a range of choices, the young person is provided with a way of coping with the situation and a way of feeling back in control

RED PHASE – STRATEGY #4

Counter-intuitive strategies

If you are not used to implementing counter-intuitive strategies (LaVigna & Willis, 1997), they can take some time to get used to! It requires us as staff to really challenge and understand what we are doing and what the bigger picture is in terms of how we are supporting the young person.

As stated already, the priority at this stage of a Challenging Behaviour Cycle is restoring order quickly and keeping people safe. This is not a stage in the cycle where new learning is going to be easily achieved for the young person, and it is not likely going to be a stage in the cycle where staff are well placed to be teaching the young person new strategies – emotions are often running high during these peak moments of crisis.

For these reasons, it can be helpful to consider using some counter-intuitive strategies – which can very quickly calm a situation and restore some order, reducing distress for the young person displaying challenging behaviour and reducing stress for staff trying to manage the situation.

They are called counter-intuitive because they are strategies that often go against our gut feelings, and which may even generate resistance and disagreement from colleagues. Any counter-intuitive strategies should always be recorded within the Coping Plan – so that these feelings can be minimised and the approaches used without staff feeling that their approach and decisions will be questioned.

The best example of an effective counter-intuitive strategy is the **introduction of tangible things that the young person likes and enjoys**. For example, if Gary is engaging in difficult behaviour (throwing resources, shouting at staff) staff may choose to offer Gary some time away from the situation to engage in one of his favourite activities or to take some time to go and play games that he particularly enjoys.

- To many staff, and quite naturally so, this feels wrong.
- It feels like something we shouldn't do.
- It feels as if we give Gary things that he wants at this point, we are reinforcing his behaviour.

Staff often have some very valid questions about using such a strategy, such as:

- Why should he get what he wants when his behaviour is so difficult?

- Why should he get nice things when other well behaved children aren't getting them?
- Won't he just behave like this more in the future so he can get his toys again?
- Surely there must be something else we can do?

It is important to justify and explain the use of counter-intuitive strategies, and the questions are answered below to frame the strategy in terms of the bigger picture and the longer-term plan we have built for supporting the young person to change their behaviour in the future.

q1. Why should he get what he wants when his behaviour is so difficult?

It's important to remember what we know about anybody presenting with challenging behaviour. That behaviour, as we have discussed elsewhere, is serving a purpose for the young person and meeting a need for them. So, if we accept that the behaviour is communicating to us that the young person **needs** something to change, then the question above could read "Why should he get what he **needs** when his behaviour is so difficult?" – and if we make this one little change to how we frame the behaviour, it can go a long way to changing our response and our attitude towards it.

Challenging behaviour is often signifying what people need, not what they want.

q2. Why should he get nice things when other well behaved children aren't getting them?

Again, it becomes important to frame our thinking about this issue in terms of what people need. Everybody needs positive affirmation of their positive behaviour. However, not everybody needs the same degree of affirmation. For most people, a small amount of acknowledgement given often is sufficient to make them feel noticed, respected, wanted, understood, heard. For other people, these reminders, and reinforcements, need to be much stronger and/or much more frequent.

When we analyse the challenging behaviour – and any patterns we have noticed have told us how often the young person needs affirmation, or needs reassurance, or needs comfort – then we can plan to provide this in the future in line with their individual needs.

Q3. Won't he just behave like this more in the future so he can get his toys again?

There is always a possibility that how we respond to challenging behaviour can make it more, or less, likely to happen again in the future. And there is a danger that a young person will make the link between a challenging behaviour they present with, and any positive consequences that happen afterwards. So, we should make sure that if we opt to use this type of strategy, if we decide to provide something enjoyable to stop an unwanted behaviour, that we also provide access to those enjoyable activities/toys/foods at times when the young person is behaving in a more acceptable manner.

The link between the challenging behaviour and the favourite activity will only be established if that is the only time the young person receives that activity.

Q4. Surely there must be something else we can do?

The short response to this is yes, there must be something else we can do. But perhaps not right now. Not now that the behaviour has got to this point. Introducing counter-intuitive strategies is a last resort strategy. It does not teach the young person any new ways to cope with the stressors they are experiencing. It is not a proactive way to respond. It simply stops the challenging behaviour at that moment. It doesn't make it less likely to happen again in the future.

The '*something else*' that we can do comes much earlier in the cycle of behaviour. It comes in the **Yellow Phase** and the **Green Phase** in the Coping Plan. It is the result of the analysis of the behaviour we build up over time and the knowledge we have of the young person's health, triggers, likes, and dislikes. So, we can certainly do something else, but it will be next time, when we notice the behaviour starting again, and it will be one of the many strategies we have described in the earlier stages of our Coping Plan.

SUMMARY OF CHAPTER 5

The Red Phase / "The Active Phase"

In this chapter, we have explored the Reactive Strategies we may have to employ if behaviour does escalate to a point of crisis or meltdown. With these management strategies in mind, it's time to complete the Red Phase, the third section of your Coping Plan.

You may have found some of the strategies discussed useful and appropriate for the young person you are supporting, or you may have decided that some alternative approaches are going to be more helpful and appropriate.

In the completed example of the Coping Plan we looked at in Chapter 2, there were 5 identified strategies at this stage of the plan. See Figure 5.3 to review them.

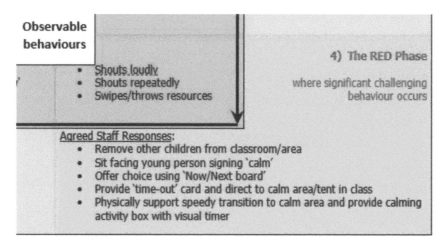

Figure 5.3 Red Phase of the Coping Plan from our completed example in Chapter 2

CHAPTER 5   REFERENCES

LaVigna, G., & Willis, T. (2005). Multi element model for breaking the barriers to social and community integration. *Tizard Learning Disability Review*, *10*(2), 16–23.

LaVigna, G.W., & Willis, T.T.J. (1997). Severe and challenging behaviour: Counter-intuitive strategies for crisis management within a non-aversive framework. *Positive Practices*, *2*(2): 1–17.

CHAPTER 6

THE BLUE PHASE / "THE RECOVERY PHASE"

STEP 6: EXPLORE AND RECORD SUITABLE REFLECTIVE STRATEGIES TO BE IMPLEMENTED AT THE BLUE PHASE

Completing the Coping Plan

Step 1: Describe Observable Behaviours

Step 2: Build up a personal profile for the young person

Step 3: Explore and record suitable Proactive Strategies to be implemented at the Yellow Phase

Step 4: Explore and record suitable Focussed Support Strategies to be implemented at the Green Phase

Step 5: Explore and record suitable Reactive Strategies to be implemented at the Red Phase

Step 6: Explore and record suitable Reflective Practices to be implemented at the Blue Phase

Step 6 of completing the Coping Plan requires an exploration of what factors will be helpful to the young person, and to staff, in the minutes and hours after an incident has occurred. At times, challenging behaviour can generate high emotional states for staff and have an impact for some staff on their own wellbeing (Jenkins *et al.*, 1997). We will explore strategies that staff can use to help the pupil, and themselves, to reflect on and learn from incidents, and to develop practice for the future.

Reflection and review

After any incidents of challenging behaviour it is essential that both the young person and staff have the opportunity to reflect on what happened and to do some purposeful planning about how things might be improved in the future.

STRATEGIES FOR REFLECTION AND REVIEW

The strategies listed here are by no means intended to represent an exhaustive list of the things you may choose to implement. Each of these strategies is provided as a starting point to provide some initial ideas for things you may wish to include within this stage of your Coping Plans.

The timing of these strategies or other similar strategies is very important. For some young people, it may be helpful to use these strategies very soon after an incident – to help them recall the events and to establish clear links between their behaviour, the consequences, and the factors that underpinned the incident.

For other young people, it may be better to wait a period of time – a cooling-off period – and then to revisit the events in a structured and calm manner, free from some of the emotion attached to the incident in question.

The **Blue Phase** strategies covered are:

- Strategy #1 – The Young Person's ABC Chart
- Strategy #2 – Positive Cycle Tool
- Strategy #3 – Stop Behaviours – Start Behaviours
- Strategy #4 – Relaxation
- Strategy #5 – Debriefing

BLUE PHASE – STRATEGY #1

The young person's ABC chart

For young people who can reflect verbally or in written form about their behaviour, the following tool can be useful to help them consider some of the elements of their behaviour cycle, and provides helpful discussion points about things that could be changed to help them cope a little better in the future. A blank chart is provided in Figure 6.1, and it contains three sections to be completed with the young person:

> **A – A**ctivating event
>
> Ask the pupil to list some of the activating events that triggered the incident.
>
> **B – B**elief (of the young person)
>
> List some of the thoughts they had while the event was taking place (or immediately before and after)
>
> **C – C**onsequences and **C**hoices
>
> And finally ask them to describe any consequences (either immediate or longer-term).
>
> The spaces in each column can be used for pupils to draw if they find this easier than writing. Also, the adult can offer to write if the pupil would rather speak their answers.

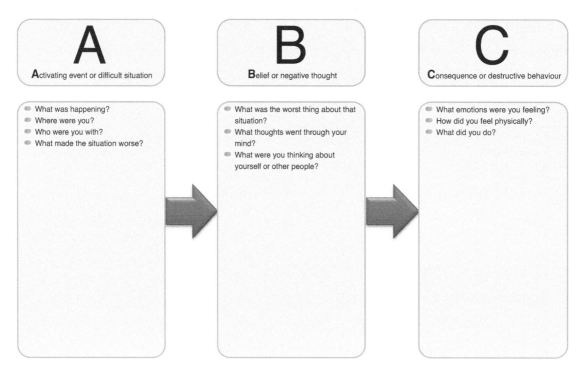

Figure 6.1 The young person's ABC chart

The process of describing and recording these things can be a helpful one in itself. However, this tool is most effective if it can be used with the Positive Cycle Tool (**Blue Phase** – Strategy #2). Using the two tools together allows the pupil to capture some specifics of what happened when things went badly and what that might mean for them (or others) in the future. Using the **Positive Cycle Tool** then gives the young person the opportunity and the support to envisage an alternative way of dealing with the same situation if it arises again – and to imagine some more positive outcomes. To use the Positive Cycle Tool alongside this ABC chart, it should be introduced after, or as part of, completing column **C**.

BLUE PHASE – STRATEGY #2

Positive Cycle Tool

The Positive Cycle Tool is a technique that draws upon the principles of Cognitive Behaviour Therapy (see Branch & Wilson, 2010 for an introduction to CBT). CBT interventions are grounded in the notion that our thoughts, feelings, and behaviour are all interrelated and all influence each other.

The intention of this technique is to help the young person to understand the link between their behaviour, their thoughts, and their feelings – and then to try to generate alternative ways of acting in similar situations in the future.

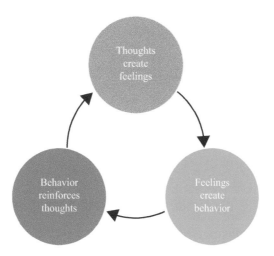

Figure 6.2 Positive Cycle Tool

Step 1 – The negative cycle

The young person will be asked to record:

- What happened – **A**ctions/The event (Behaviour)
- What they thought at the time – **B**eliefs (Thoughts)
- What choices they made and any resulting feelings – **C**onsequences & **C**hoices (Feelings)

---

*If you have already used the young person's ABC chart (**Blue Phase** – Strategy #1) you may well have this information already and can jump ahead to step 2.*

Step 2 – The positive cycle

In step 2, the adult is going to guide the young person through a process of imagining alternative endings for similar situations by systematically talking about the young person's feelings after the event and the choices they made (or the behaviour they presented) which created those feelings.

The adult will write down the event that was discussed in Step 1, above:

- What happened – **A**ctions/The event (Behaviour)

The young person will then be asked to record:

- What they thought at the time – **B**eliefs (Thoughts)

The young person will then be asked to generate 3 alternative choices they could have made:

- What other choices they could make in future, and any resulting feelings – **C**onsequences & **C**hoices (Feelings)

After each new choice is expressed by the young person, the adult will ask the young person how that might have changed the outcome and how it may have created different feelings for the young person.

The hope is that the young person will be encouraged to recognise the link between any negative feelings or emotions they have experienced, and the choices or behaviour that led up to those emotions. Once this link is established, the adult and the young person will have a shared dialogue and a narrative about similar events in future that can be used to focus attention on the positive outcomes that could be achieved by the choices (behaviour) that are made.

This strategy will be more successful for young people with high levels of emotional literacy. For young people who struggle to recognise feelings, or to name emotions, it may be necessary to undertake some additional work (in the Yellow Phase) around developing emotional literacy and boosting the young person's ability to recognise, name, and respond to their own emotions and feelings.

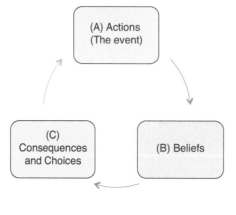

Figure 6.3 Positive Cycle Tool Step 1: When things went badly (negative cycle)

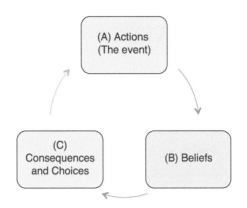

Figure 6.4 Positive Cycle Tool Step 2: How things might change (positive cycle)

BLUE PHASE – STRATEGY #3

Stop behaviours – start behaviours

Over time, once the young person has been given the opportunity to reflect with an adult on several episodes of unwanted behaviour, it may be helpful for the young person to begin keeping a log of positive alternative behaviours they have identified.

A simple table like Table 6.1 can be helpful when reflecting on incidents. It keeps a rolling record of the alternative positive behaviours that the young person and supporting adults would like to encourage.

Table 6.1 Sample record of stop behaviours – start behaviours

Stop Behaviours (The unwanted behaviour) →	Start Behaviours (A healthier alternative)
Running out of the classroom	Pass the teacher an 'Exit Card'
Rocking backward on my chair	Use my wibble cushion and foot rest
Ripping up my work	Use my Scribble Pad when I get frustrated

6

Table 6.2 Record of stop behaviours – start behaviours

Stop Behaviours	⟶ Start Behaviours

During reflection sessions this list can be reviewed between the young person and supporting adult. The blank version of this chart in Table 6.2 can be used to develop a range of behaviours that have been identified as healthier, positive alternatives.

This type of list can be used as a rolling record shared with the young person and added to whenever new strategies are identified. The strategies generated here will also become new strategies used in the Yellow Phase and **Green Phase** of the Coping Plan and should be added to it as soon as they are identified.

BLUE PHASE – STRATEGY #4

6

Relaxation – an overview

We have talked elsewhere about challenging behaviour being a form of communication and that often that communication is that the young person isn't coping well with a situation as a result of stress, anxiety, or being overwhelmed. For this reason, it can be very helpful if staff can find opportunities to help the young person to relax. Indeed, teaching the young person how to relax may well be the first necessary step in this endeavour.

Relaxation techniques may need to be taught during the Yellow Phase when the young person will be more able to take on board new learning and internalise the use of these strategies. But once they have been demonstrated effectively, the **Blue Phase** is an ideal opportunity to introduce some relaxation strategies as one way of helping the young person to cope and reduce their levels of stress or anxiety.

The following pages will outline different strategies for guided relaxation that adults can help the young person to use. There are lots of techniques to choose from when developing relaxation and breathing strategies for young people, and it is often helpful to co-develop scripts and techniques with the young person to make them more meaningful and personal. The example techniques covered here are:

- Progressive Muscle Relaxation
- Visualisation
- Milkshake Breathing

Relaxation – progressive muscle relaxation

The following script is used to help the young person systematically relax muscles throughout their body. Set aside approximately 10 minutes to undertake this activity.

Get ready

- Find a quiet space.
- Don't try to do this relaxation exercise if you are short on time.
- Don't do this after eating, as it might be difficult if you are full up.

Time to relax

- Sit comfortably.

- Tense each of the following muscle groups for about *5 seconds* each and relax for *10 seconds* each:

  (1) Right hand and lower arm – make a tight fist (5 seconds). Then relax (10 seconds).

  (2) Right upper arm – pull your elbow against your hip bone. Then relax.

  (3) Left hand and lower arm – make a tight fist. Then relax.

  (4) Left upper arm – pull your elbow against your hip bone. Then relax.

  (5) Forehead – frown. Then relax.

  (6) Eyes – screw up your eyes tight. Then relax. When you relax, leave them closed.

  (7) Jaw – clench your teeth and pull back the corners of your mouth. Then relax.

  (8) Neck – push your chin down. Then relax.

  (9) Shoulders and upper back – take a deep breath in, hunch your shoulders. Then relax, letting your breathing become slow and regular as you do it.

  (10) Stomach – tense the muscles of your stomach. Then relax.

  (11) Right thigh – concentrate on tensing both the muscles at the front and the ones behind the thigh. Then relax.

  (12) Right calf – point your toes upwards. Then relax.

  (13) Right foot – curl your toes. Then relax.

  (14) Left thigh – concentrate on tensing both the muscles at the front and the ones behind the thigh. Then relax.

  (15) Left calf – point your toes upwards. Then relax.

  (16) Left foot – curl your toes. Then relax.

Relaxation – visualisation

Set aside about 5 minutes to use this script with the young person. (When you have time you could develop a more personalised script with the young person.)

For a few moments, focus on your breathing. Allow your breathing to relax you. Breathe in . . . and out. In . . . out. . . . In . . . Out. . . .

Continue to breathe slowly and peacefully; feel the tension starting to leave your body.

Continue to let your breathing relax you. . . . Breathe in . . . 2 . . . 3 . . . 4 . . . hold . . . 2 . . . 3 . . . out . . . 2 . . . 3 . . . 4 . . . 5.

Let your breathing become slower and relax. Now begin to create a picture in your mind of a place where you can completely relax. Imagine what this place needs to be like in order for you to feel calm and relaxed.

Start with what the place looks like. . . . Where is this peaceful place? Is it outdoors . . . or indoors? . . . Is it a small place or is it big? (pause)

Now think about who is in this place? Are you alone? Is someone else with you? Are there animals? (pause)

Focus now on what you can see – the colours, shapes . . . objects. . . .plants . . . water . . . all of the things that make your place enjoyable.

Picture yourself in this peaceful place. Imagine a feeling of calm . . . of peace . . . a place where you have no worries, cares, or concerns . . . a place where you can simply rejuvenate, relax, and enjoy just being. (pause)

Enjoy your peaceful place for a few moments more. In these last few moments of relaxation, create a picture in your mind that you will return to the next time you need a quick relaxation break. Picture yourself in your peaceful place.

When you are ready to return to your day, turn your attention back to the present. Notice your surroundings as your body and mind return to their usual level of alertness and wakefulness.

Relaxation – milkshake breathing

Milkshake breathing can be a really helpful and fun technique to get young people focusing on their deep breathing. Deep breathing can then become a strategy that the young person uses independently or with adult support whenever they notice that they are becoming overwhelmed, stressed, or anxious.

Young people will very often find deep breathing difficult until they are taught how to do it.

Figure 6.5 Breathe like you're making bubbles in a milkshake

To teach deep breathing using the milkshake technique:

- You need a glass filled one quarter full with water.
- Ask the young person to blow some bubbles in the water using a straw.
- Then ask them to keep the straw in the water, and breathe in through their nose, counting to 3.
- Ask them to hold that breath for 3 seconds.
- Then ask them to breathe out slowly for 3 seconds, making more bubbles in the water.

You can repeat this exercise as many times as necessary within the Yellow Phase until the young person has mastered the steps of taking a deep breath through their nose, holding it, and then deeply exhaling.

Once the young person has mastered this technique, adults can remind them to use their deep breathing at any point when they are beginning to feel overwhelmed. Adults can also use deep breathing with the young person in the **Blue Phase** when the young person is being supported to reflect upon incidents or return to their scheduled activities immediately after an incident.

BLUE PHASE – STRATEGY #5

Debriefing

Debriefing is a responsive strategy which is used after incidents of challenging behaviour to support the staff involved. There are two aspects of debriefing after incidents of challenging behaviour. The first involves emotional support for staff to reduce stress. The second aspect involves reviewing practice to ensure lessons are learnt and practice can be modified if necessary in future.

1. Emotional support for staff

Supporting young people who present with challenging behaviour can at times be emotionally very draining for staff – as well as being highly rewarding at other times!

Ensuring that staff have access to adequate processes for debriefing after incidents of challenging behaviour is crucial to protect the emotional wellbeing of staff, so that they are able to continue providing effective support for the young person.

The nature of this 'debriefing' will vary from setting to setting and each member of staff will have different preferences in terms of what their 'debrief' looks like. The debrief may be a formal process or it may be more informal.

For some staff, it is enough to continue with the usual routine of the day once the incident has passed. For others, a few minutes away from the situation may be necessary, perhaps with a cup of tea in the staff room. For other staff, it may be important that they have some time with a colleague to talk through the incident.

2. Reviewing practice

> "Where there are shared understandings about challenging behaviour, practice became more consistent and challenging behaviour reduced"
>
> (Lavan, 2012, p. 100)

The second key purpose for debriefing is to develop practice to ensure that the young person is supported effectively in the future.

At this final stage of the Coping Plan it is important that staff take time to review the Coping Plan and to consider any adaptations that may be necessary. The assess-plan-do-review cycle outlined back in Chapter 1 comes full circle at this point as staff undertake the formal process of 'reviewing' the plan they have in place and returning to the 'assess' stage, where they ask the questions:

- Has this incident taught us anything new about the function of the behaviour?
- Have we used any new strategies successfully that should be added to the Coping Plan?
- Were any new behaviours presented, particularly 'warning' behaviours at the **Green Phase**?

In answering questions such as this, staff will be able to make necessary adjustments to the Coping Plan with the hope that these refinements will further increase the likelihood that the young person is going to develop better means of coping with the things they are finding difficult and that future incidents will be managed successfully, reducing stress for the young person and for staff involved.

SUMMARY OF CHAPTER 6

The Blue Phase / "The Recovery Phase"

Now that we have considered some of the aspects that will be helpful for the young person and for staff in reflecting upon the behaviour being presented, it's time to complete the Blue Phase, the final section of your Coping Plan.

You may have found some of the strategies discussed useful and appropriate for the young person you are supporting, or you may have decided that some alternative approaches are going to be more helpful and appropriate.

In the completed example of the Coping Plan we looked at in Chapter 2, there were 3 identified strategies at this stage of the plan. See Figure 6.6 to review them.

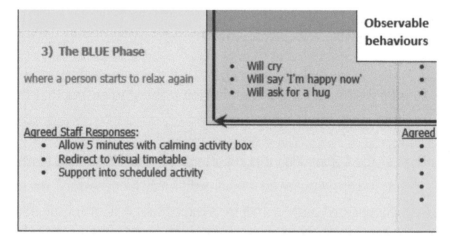

Figure 6.6 Blue Phase of the Coping Plan from our completed example in Chapter 2

CHAPTER 6   REFERENCES

Branch, R., & Wilson, R. (2010). *Cognitive behavioural therapy for dummies*. London: Wiley.

Jenkins, R., Rose, J., & Lovell, C. (1997). Psychological well-being of staff working with people who have challenging behaviour. *Journal of Learning Disability Research*, *41*, 502–511.

Lavan, G. (2012). SPACE: An integrative framework for creating capable environments for behaviour which challenges. Unpublished Doctoral Thesis, Paper in Draft, Exeter University.

CHAPTER 7

BEYOND THE COPING PLAN

The final chapter will reflect on the process of using the Coping Plan and the journey of behaviour change. This chapter will also explore how the Coping Plan fits in the wider context of support for challenging behaviour, considering other ways that staff can support improvements in wellbeing for the young person by developing their understanding of the influences on behaviour from within:

- The young person
- Their family
- The wider community

In conclusion, Chapter 7 will provide advice about other sources of support, such as national charities.

SUMMARY OF THIS BOOK

Throughout this book we have explored how challenging behaviour always acts as a communication of need, often serving the function of helping people to feel more in control of their environment and better able to predict what is going to happen next. A known pattern of challenging behaviour and predictable responses from adults is often less stress-inducing than a lesson or situation where the young person can't predict what will happen next and can't control whether they will be asked to do things they find difficult.

Some of the key principles and questions we have covered:

- All behaviour is a form of communication
- What factors drive or underpin the behaviour?
- What purpose is it serving?
- Having a 'best guess', formulating an explanation, and devising a plan

The Coping Plan and this book provide a framework and a **practical guide** to offer you, as staff, ways to make sense of and understand unwanted behaviour and plan how to support a young person effectively. We have seen that one way to try to understand challenging behaviour is to frame it as the result of a person's **fight/ flight/freeze** instincts being triggered, and we have mapped out the different phases of the Challenging Behaviour Cycle. The box summarises the key elements of the framework we have explored.

Chapter 1-2   The first challenge is to understand challenging behaviour. To do so, we examined:

- Some **evolutionary** and biological explanations for challenging behaviour
- An **Iceberg Model** of challenging behaviour
- A **flowchart** for exploring why behaviour happens, and some possible strategy starting points
- The **Challenging Behaviour Cycle**
- The **Coping Plan** document

Chapter 3   The most important phase for developing support is the Yellow Phase. It is here that staff can develop the **preventative** and **Proactive Strategies** that will ultimately help the young person to develop **new coping skills** and prevent the need for the young person to engage in challenging behaviour to have their needs met.

Chapter 4   In the Green Phase we explored **Focussed Support Strategies** and how staff can **intervene** when unwanted behaviour begins to present. At this phase we highlighted the importance of **spotting patterns of behaviour**, recording these, and analysing them so that we can be more proactive in the future and use the knowledge from these patterns to inform our understanding of the behaviour.

Chapter 5   We then looked at what to do in the Red Phase, when challenging behaviour reaches peak levels. The priority of any **Reactive Strategies** at this phase is to restore order quickly, and keep everybody safe if behaviour becomes dangerous.

Chapter 6   After incidents of challenging behaviour, both the young person and staff will need the opportunity to do some purposeful **reflection** and planning about how things might be improved in the future. In the Blue Phase we looked at how to ensure that we adhere to the principles of an **assess-plan-do-review** approach.

A WIDER CONTEXT

In using the Coping Plan we have begun the process of planning for some of the most immediate and pressing behaviours and challenges that are presented within our school or setting. However, it is important to remain focused on the fact that there are factors from outside of our setting of which we will have very limited knowledge and factors that may be fundamental to the development and maintenance of challenging behaviour that are beyond our control.

All behaviour exists within a context which includes the young person, their family, their school, their community, and the wider world.

At each level there are risk and protective factors which will make it more, or less, likely that a person will present with challenging behaviour in response to difficulties they encounter. The table on the next page summarises some of the key risk factors at each of three key levels. The more risk factors that are present for our young person, the more likely it is that they will experience difficulties with coping, have reduced wellbeing, and present with challenging behaviours.

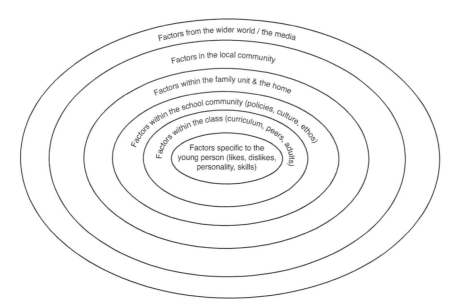

Figure 7.1 The many contexts of behaviour

These wider issues are introduced here because many are fundamental to the development and maintenance of challenging behaviour and may even be beyond our reach in terms of making immediate positive changes for the young person we are supporting.

Table 7.1 Risk and protective factors

Risk Factors in the Young Person/School	Risk Factors in the Family/Home	Risk Factors in the Wider Community
• Specific learning difficulties • Communication difficulties • Specific developmental delay • Genetic influence • Difficult temperament • Physical illness (especially if chronic and/or neurological) • Academic failure • Low self-esteem	• Overt parental conflict • Family breakdown • Inconsistent or unclear discipline • Hostile or rejecting relationships • Failure to adapt to a child's changing needs • Neglect • Physical, sexual or emotional abuse • Parental psychiatric illness • Parental criminality, alcoholism or substance misuse • Death and loss – including loss of friendship	• Socio-economic disadvantage • Homelessness • Disaster • Discrimination • Hostile, rejecting or abusive relationships • Lack of child rearing practice • Lack of rehabilitation opportunities • Other significant life events
Developing Resilience to These Influences:		
• Provide children with a secure base • Cultivate a sense of belonging • Provide responsible and reliable relationships	• Develop a sense of the child's worthiness and competence • Develop a sense of efficacy through problem solving and planning skills	• Develop self-awareness/self-efficacy

Table adapted from (Gilligan, 1997).

Many research studies have claimed to demonstrate superiority of one approach for challenging behaviour over many others. However, challenging behaviour is a complex phenomenon and there appears to be little agreement generally as to whether any approaches can claim superiority over other approaches studied. A study by the Royal College of Psychiatrists *et al.* (2007) concluded that severe challenging behaviour "is likely to lead to responses that are restrictive, aversive or result in exclusion" (p. 10). Numerous studies have concluded that no one approach is suitable for all individuals or for the same individual across time and that 'eclectic provision' (Parsons *et al.*, 2009) is the ideal.

The Coping Plan we have explored in this text is one tool we can utilise to help us better manage unwanted behaviour, incorporating a range of strategies and interventions, in order to help the young person cope better with difficult situations and develop healthier responses in the future.

The work we do at this individual level is vital, and should not be minimised in any way. But it should also sit within this wider understanding of what the young person needs. On the following pages is an outline of the SPACE Framework (Lavan, 2012), which places the Coping Plan as one element within the context of other equally important factors and activities required at the school, family, and community levels.

The SPACE Framework was developed over several years' working with special schools in the UK for young people who present with challenging behaviour and

Figure 7.2 The SPACE Framework (Lavan, 2012)

autism spectrum conditions. The research identified 5 key areas of support that led to effective support for challenging behaviour, one of which was the use of detailed written plans, such as the Coping Plan. The 5 key areas are summarised in the figure on the previous page, and an overview of each is provided below.

Supporting staff

Staff need support in three key ways

1. Through Training and Psycho-education
   - All staff benefit from regular training in behaviour. Not short one-off sessions, but a long-term or ongoing programme.
   - Staff should receive training in a wide range of evidence-based practices.
2. Emotional Management
   - Staff need access to carefully planned emotional support and debriefing in response to serious incidents and also in response to the psychological impact of supporting young people with emotional difficulties.
3. Functional Behaviour Assessment (see Jordan, 2001)
   - Staff should have regular opportunities to discuss, as a team the reason why unwanted behaviour happens – and to develop a written, shared understanding of the behaviour. This is fundamental to delivery of a consistent approach.

Personalised Coping Plan

- Intervention and strategies should be evidence-informed – why are approaches/ strategies being selected?
- A range of approaches should be utilised to provide 'eclectic provision' (Parsons *et al.*, 2009).
- Strategies should be linked to specific goals/targets/skill development.

Active involvement of families

- Families must be involved in developing plans and in prioritising skills to be developed through selected strategies.
- Schools should look to incorporate strategies used by the family at home.

Collaborative multi-agency working

- Meetings and sharing of information should be used to coordinate multi-agency working.
- The goal of multi-agency working is to increase consistency across settings and to reduce demands on families.

Effective monitoring and review

- Systematic collection, analysis, and review of data is essential.
- To support and ensure evidence-based practice, decisions about changes to personalised Coping Plans should be objective (informed by data) rather than subjective (informed by opinion/preference) where possible.

In using the Coping Plan we have become more systematic in how we approach challenging behaviour. Thinking more deeply about **why behaviour occurs** is the first and most crucial part of becoming more **systematic** in our support. Incidents of challenging behaviour cannot be viewed as random, out-of-the-blue events that arise 'from nowhere'. They very rarely, if ever, are. The triggers for challenging behaviour can sometimes be immediate things within the environment, but often they will result from gradual build-up over time of numerous stressors and pressures that the young person is struggling to cope with.

Understanding the young person by building up and developing our profile of them can aid us in our efforts to understand both the immediate triggers and the wider factors involved. We have seen that evolutionary perspectives and biological factors can explain some of the key drivers for challenging behaviour, and that there can be numerous influences lurking 'beneath the surface' of our iceberg – meaning that **behaviour always occurs for a reason**, and unwanted behaviour is exactly the same.

Hopefully, using the principles outlined in this book, and the framework described, we will be able to consider the factors contributing to unwanted behaviour and to make effective changes to help young people cope better, improve their experience of school, and ultimately improve their quality of life.

SOURCES OF SUPPORT, ADVICE, AND OTHER USEFUL LINKS

The Challenging Behaviour Foundation
www.challengingbehaviour.org.uk/

Institute of Applied Behaviour Analysis
www.iaba.com/#

National Autistic Society
www.nas.org.uk/about/behaviour/challenging-behaviour.aspx

Psychology Training Hub
www.psychologytraininghub.com/challenging-behaviour

Your Psychology
www.yourpsychology.co.uk/

CHAPTER 7   REFERENCES

Department of Health (2009). *Valuing people now: A new strategy for people with learning disabilities.* London: TSO.

Gilligan, R. (1997). Beyond permanence? The importance of resilience in child placement practice and planning. *Adoption & Fostering, 21*(1), 12–20.

Jordan, R. (2001). *Autism with severe learning difficulties.* London: Souvenir Press.

Lavan, G. (2012). SPACE: An integrative framework for creating capable environments for behaviour which challenges. Unpublished Doctoral Thesis, Paper in Draft, Exeter University.

Parsons, S., Guldberg, K., MacLeod, A., & Jones, G. (2009). *International review of the literature of evidence of best practice provision in the education of persons with autistic spectrum disorders.* NCSE, Dublin.

Royal College of Psychiatrists, British Psychological Society and Royal College of Speech and Language Therapists (2007). *Challenging behaviour a unified approach – Clinical and service guidelines for supporting people with learning disabilities who are at risk of receiving abusive or restrictive practices.* London: RCPsy, BPS, RCSLT.